Secret Keys
to a
STEM Degree

The Wisdom I Wish I Had While Pursuing an Engineering Degree

Justin Rittenhouse, PhD

Formats Available:
ISBN: 979-8-9931757-0-6 (eBook)
ISBN: 979-8-9931757-1-3 (Softcover)
ISBN: 979-8-9931757-2-0 (Hardcover)

Library of Congress Control Number: 2025920551
Published in St. Joseph, Michigan

Editors: Danielle Rittenhouse, Eric L. Thomas
Cover Design by: Getcovers

This book is dedicated to my lovely wife, **Danielle Rittenhouse**, our beautiful daughter, **Eva Rittenhouse**, and our future children.

In addition, this book is in loving memory of my Grandma,
Barbara Clous.

Contents

Contents

1. Introduction

1.1. Author's biography

Justin Rittenhouse has an elaborate background in STEM, including high levels of success in academics and industry. Academically, he has earned a PhD in mechanical engineering, subsequent to a master's and a bachelor's degree in aerospace engineering. He attended Western Michigan University (WMU), where he taught during graduate school. Later, he became a full-time faculty member at Mount Vernon Nazarene University (MVNU). His main foci are mechanical engineering and computer science. In these fields, he accumulated intern, co-op, and full-time engineering experience, including serving as an engineering manager. His unusual path has taught him many lessons along the way. The hope is this book can help students avoid learning many of these lessons the hard way, like he did. For more information about his credentials, please visit his website: JustinRittenhousePhD.com.

1.2. My path to a STEM degree

My path to college was different than most since I did not go to college right after high school. In fact, going to college wasn't even a part of my plans. I coasted through high school maintaining a B average while never doing homework or putting in any real effort. In addition, I didn't really know anyone who went to college; perhaps an aunt or uncle, but no one I knew well or talked to. Certainly, there was no one I knew well enough to have a big enough impact on my life to change my thought process. At this point, you're probably wondering how I went from an average high school student to a PhD in what many would call a difficult field. Well, have you ever stocked groceries or faced shelves (pulling product forward on the shelf to make it look good) for eight hours a day? If not, don't as facing is atrocious. I say this from experience, since my first non-temp job after high school was being a stocker. I ended up stocking all the way through undergrad. While I cannot recall the exact day or my exact age, I do distinctly remember the exact moment I decided to go to college and probably will for the rest of my life. I was standing in the back of the grocery store where I worked, between two bay doors holding a pallet and standing on another, waiting for the milk truck driver to arrive. The only thoughts crossing my mind in that moment were how awful that job was, and that I had to do something different, anything! There was no way I could do that job for another 50 years, at least not happily. That moment in time completely changed my trajectory. That moment brought me to writing this book. Without that moment, you would not be reading this sentence, and my life would have been completely different. Thankfully, that moment did happen and here we are!

People often ask why I chose engineering; truthfully, I don't have a good answer. I wish I had some amazing backstory about inventing some cool gadget as a toddler, and then my passion for engineering grew from there. But, that simply isn't how my story goes. I actually started college as a business major, and during my first semester it became apparent all my friends were engineering majors. While most of my memories from back then have faded, I suppose that's why I switched, which, honestly, is a poor reason to switch majors. Making the decision even worse is the fact I've lost contact with everyone in that friend group and don't believe anyone else actually finished the degree. Luckily, that decision to switch still ended up being wise.

Looking back at my past school successes, I should have known being an engineer was my calling card as I typically did exceptionally well in math. This "natural" K–12 math ability likely stems from doing math for fun. The best example of this was in 3rd grade where I regularly did long division for fun. The class would be watching a movie, and I would be doing long division. Sometimes at recess, I would stay in and do long division. My 3rd grade teacher even gave me a toy car in front of the class as a reward for all my hard work. Thus, had I been wiser, I would have known the whole time I was destined to earn a STEM (Science, Technology, Engineering, and Mathematics) degree.

At the end of the day, I fully recommend your decision to pursue a STEM degree. It will be one of the best decisions of your life. With all the knowledge I've gain so far, if I could go back in time and reselect a major, STEM would still be my preference. Though, I'm not sure if I would stick with engineering, as computer science also appeals to me; it's definitely a difficult choice to make.

1.3. The main purpose of this book

The goal of this book is to pass along the information I wish I had before adventuring on (and during) my STEM path, thus helping to ensure that future generations will have an easier path than mine. The target audience is anyone pursuing a STEM degree, from high school to college students, including non-traditional students. The earlier you are in your STEM path, the better this book will be able to help you. My background is in aerospace/mechanical engineering; this book is slightly geared in that direction. However, most of the information holds true for other STEM majors. This book is not meant to teach you how to be an engineer (or any other STEM major). It will not cover complex engineering problems or how to solve them. You have many more years of school ahead of you for that, enjoy :). This book is meant to be concise and yet still provide a wealth of information NOT taught (or skimmed over) in school. Also, I strongly encourage you to checkout my website, JustinRittenhousePhD.com, as I plan on updating it regularly with resources that you may find beneficial.

Note that there is a bullet point list at the end of every chapter and a place to write a few notes. Use it! In essence, embrace *active* reading; take notes directly in the book! In the future, instead of rereading whole sections, you can quickly refer to the list and your notes for a quick reminder of the information you were seeking. Though, rereading the whole section is recommended when the related information is most useful. For example, if you are preparing for an interview, it would be beneficial to reread section 5.6. As an aside, active reading is a skill you should develop if you haven't already, and you should use it when reading for information (e.g., this book or textbooks). This means writing in the margins, highlighting important information, etc. If you don't want to annotate directly in the book, taking notes elsewhere would work as well, such as a notepad. Essentially, do whatever you need to do to improve your comprehension of the material.

Lastly, remember to never give up on your dreams; I took longer than average to get a bachelor's degree. I took longer than average to get a master's degree. I took longer than average to get a PhD. Who cares? I did it my way and worked many jobs the whole way through. There are no dates or timestamps on a degree. If it takes you longer than most to earn a bachelor's degree, so what? You still earned the degree. As of 2019, that's a claim only about $\frac{1}{3}$ of those 25 years or older can make within the United States.[1] No one knows your whole story or the challenges you faced. Don't let people deter you because your path isn't the path they think you should take; keep grinding and never give up!

Chapter Bullet Points

- I was not an amazing high school student

- My background is in aerospace/mechanical engineering and computer science, and my biases lean in that direction

- This book is for STEM majors (including high schoolers)

- There is no date on a degree

Notes

_____

_____

_____

_____

_____

_____

2. Is college right for you?

Depending on what crowd you find yourself in, you will either hear college is a fantastic idea and everyone should attend, or college is an horrible idea and no one should be stuck with the inevitable burden known as student loan debt. Like normal with a pair of opposing claims, the truth lies somewhere in between. Of course, college isn't right for everyone. Nonetheless, if you plan on working in a STEM field, college is probably the safer choice. In this chapter, we will outline why you should go to college, and why you shouldn't. As always, do not be afraid to ask for guidance. This book is designed to be a helpful tool and to assist in out of the box thinking. However, it is impossible for me to personally know you, and the nuances of your life. Therefore, it is important to bounce ideas off of someone you trust (e.g., a parent or teacher). In addition, do not hesitate to reach out to multiple people. It is actually preferred that you reach out to a few different resources. This allows for different viewpoints. For most of our early life, often into our twenties, we have a habit of putting people close to us on pedestals, especially those with power over us (e.g., parents or teachers), and we act as if they're all-knowing. They're not and they can (and will) be wrong. They're only human. By no means am I trying to imply they are neither intelligent nor helpful. If they are close to you, their advice is incredibly helpful and should hold weight in your thought process. The point is, as humans, none of us are all knowing and everyone has a limited amount of knowledge. Hence, the importance of having more than one viewpoint, as the extra viewpoints allow YOU to make a better decision for YOUR future. This is ultimately YOUR decision because it is YOUR future! This means, good or bad, the only person to blame is the person in the mirror.

2.1. Why you should go to college

As a STEM major, jobs are bountiful with a college degree. All of my engineering friends were able to receive job offers after graduation, typically within just a couple of months regardless of their GPA. It's worth noting, I had a wide range of friends, and as a result, GPAs were all over the map including in the low 2s (on a 4.0 scale). On average, my friends with the higher GPAs were able to receive job offers faster and with more well-known companies. Regardless, all were able to secure a salary well above the wages of my non-college friends. Specifically, my friends who earned a bachelor's degree consistently received job offers in the range of $55,000–$65,000 in a low cost of living area (back in 2015) while my non-college friends who were also in their early twenties made between $10,000–$20,000. I also observed my friends with an engineering degree had their wages grow at a faster rate than all of my other friends. And not just faster than my non-college friends, but also faster than my friends with a bachelor's degree in a non-STEM field. While the sample size here is small (i.e., the people I know), these numbers are easily backed with additional research. With regard to wages with and without a bachelor's degree, the National Center for Education Statistics in 2019 states the median income of those with a bachelor's degree was 59% higher than those who only completed high school.[2] While this could be broken down further for the type of bachelor's degree received (e.g., STEM versus non-STEM), it should be abundantly clear earning a bachelor's degree, on average, should significantly increase your income.

One should also be mindful that most companies won't hire you without a bachelor's degree. This is because the degree informs companies that you (probably) have a foundation built in that field. This means companies won't have to train you from the ground up. The degree should save them a lot of time and money. And if you're worried that companies may think you're an expert because you have a bachelor's degree, don't be. No one thinks someone with zero years of experience is an expert, and companies know that entry-level employees still require a significant amount of training. The bachelor's degree just gets you standing; you still have a while until you're able to run.

Whether you agree with this thinking or not, does not actually matter. The job market clearly values a bachelor's degree. If you don't believe me, go on any job searching website and start looking for jobs in a STEM field that interests in. You'll find most say a bachelor's degree is required, while a few may state: "a bachelor's degree is required or X years of relevant work experience." However, if you are reading this, you probably don't have any years of relevant work experience and relevant work experience takes significantly longer to obtain than it appears. Typically, you'll find employers are looking for 5–10 years of relevant work experience in lieu of a bachelor's degree. On the surface, this can seem like the better route as a bachelor's degree in engineering is often considered a five-year degree. Therefore, it appears you can just work and be eligible for the same job opportunities as your counterparts who went to college in approximately the same time frame. In addition, you'll be producing an income and avoiding student loan debt. It sounds nice;

although, what you are not counting is time spent working your way up. Without a bachelor's degree, you most likely won't be able to get a job that is relevant to your field of interest. What you will have to do is start out as a lower-level employee and put in years of hard work, showing your worth and your capabilities. Then, your company just may be willing to let you perform duties similar to an entry-level STEM position. Your 5–10 years of relevant work experience will start at this point, and not your hire date with the company. Though, this is simply theoretical and there is no guarantee your company will give you a shot without a bachelor's degree. If they are willing to promote you, the process of working your way up can take years (if not decades). And since you will be starting your actual career later in life, the disparity in your career earnings will likely make college seem like a bargain. To sum it up, earning a bachelor's degree will probably save you a significant amount of time and money.

The good news is any bachelor's degree is far better than none. Ideally, you want a bachelor's degree in your field of interest, but companies often list equivalent bachelor's degrees that they would consider for the opening. Often, a mechanical engineering position will list a degree in mathematics, physics, or related engineering fields as an equivalent bachelor's degree they would consider in lieu of a mechanical engineering degree. Therefore, even if you choose to earn a degree in mathematics, you can still change your mind and apply for mechanical engineering roles. However, you would have a disadvantage against those with a mechanical engineering degree, so you may have to show some exceptional ability during the hiring interviews to make yourself stand out. Nevertheless, the point remains the same: a degree in mathematics will not stop you from receiving job offers for mechanical engineering roles, even without relevant work experience.

To elaborate a bit more on the fact that any bachelor's degree can occasionally be considered good enough, it is important to note quality engineers commonly don't have a STEM degree. However, it is uncommon for quality engineers to not have a bachelor's degree at all. These type of roles get filled with non-STEM majors because they often do not require technical hard skills (e.g., coding or using CAD). Nevertheless, employers still want candidates to possess a bachelor's degree. Employers often feel those with a bachelor's degree typically have improved soft skills over non-bachelor's degree candidates, such as writing and verbal communication skills.

To drive home the point that any bachelor's degree is better than none, consider this common phrase: "I have a degree, but it was a waste of money because I don't use it." Now, consider the people you've heard say that. How many of them have at least a decent job requiring soft skills, such as writing and communication? Thus, I would argue that those people are using their degree, and what they meant to say is, "My career is not in the area of my major." This is because it's significantly harder to land an office job, to earn a promotion, or to land any well-paying career that doesn't require hard physical labor without a bachelor's degree. So while someone's career may not align with their major, many who believe they "wasted their money" would not have the careers they do have without a bachelor's degree, and they would probably be working a minimum wage job without it.

Another advantage of college is the ability to explore different career options. While this benefit may seem minor to some, 35% of STEM students do end up switching their majors within three years of enrolling.[3] This is one area where I failed, as I was never active in any of the available academic clubs. But, you should learn from my mistake and find ways to work with other majors, so you'll receive a feel for what other majors do. You may just find a new passion and end up changing majors, too. More information on selecting the right major is discussed in Chapter 4.

College is also a great way to start developing a network of people with similar career goals as yourself. This network can be crucial to your own long-term career. According to research by LinkedIn, in 2016 70% of job seekers were hired at companies were they already had a connection.[4] In the business world, it can often be who you know rather than what you know. That is why having a strong network can advance your career faster than trying to do everything on your own. In addition, a strong network can significantly improve your skills, as competition breeds greatness. Having skilled friends helps in numerous ways. They offer a point of contact when stuck on a problem and can provide random tips to improve your skill level faster, such as new methods or techniques you have not discovered yet. Most importantly, they could provide a new standard for you to reach. This is very common in sports; someone becomes a big fish in a small pond, and then they settle. They assume, incorrectly, that they have reached the top since they are better than everyone they know. But they need to realize everyone they know is an incredibly small sample size of the level of talent that exists. For that reason, it is best to grow your network of people from all walks of life to see a much broader scope of talent. Hence the importance of college. Not only do you receive a broad scope of students, but you also get a broad scope of professors to add to your network.

An additional benefit of developing a network in college is connecting with individuals who are developing different skills. For instance, if you are planning on being an entrepreneur, knowing a marketing and/or business major to bounce ideas off of would be highly beneficial, as few start-ups are done alone. The average number of members in a start-up is four.[5] One last advantage is that colleges typically provide the essentials (housing, food, power, etc.), making college a fantastic first step for many young adults who are gaining independence and financial responsibility for the first time.

2.2. Why you shouldn't go to college

The obvious answer of why you shouldn't go to college is to avoid college debt. However, avoiding debt to work a minimum wage job your whole life isn't the answer. You need to find a way to avoid college debt and still obtain a fulfilling career. There are several alternative paths to achieve this.

The very best would be to pursue your own passions and ideas. What is often forgotten is college is always there. Colleges have been around for hundreds of years; they're not going anywhere. If you have an idea, give it a shot. If your idea fails, then go to college. Is starting college at age 20 instead of 18 really going to derail your life? Probably not. Don't let fear limit your success! As far as being an entrepreneur, I can't give much advice here. This isn't a book on entrepreneurship. However, I will remind you to do your due diligence before spending time (and potentially money) on a project. The only true advice I can give you is to understand your knowledge is highly limited. I promise you know way less than you think you do. This isn't a knock on you at all and it applies to all humans. It's just a statement of fact. Until you gain experience, you won't realize how little you actually knew. To expand your knowledge, research entrepreneurship, read a few books, and, if possible, talk to a trusted advisor with experience in entrepreneurship. Ask them how they did it and what tips they have for you (e.g., what pitfalls to avoid). You'll undoubtedly still make many mistakes. Therefore, understand that companies and ideas start with people making endless mistakes. Truth be told, you'll always make mistakes; they're just a part of life. Often, they should be considered as nothing more than learning opportunities. Nevertheless, doing your homework can help you avoid many of the common mistakes and pitfalls others have made. Lastly, remember to not get deterred easily. If success as an entrepreneur was easy, everyone would do it.

Another reason to avoid college, especially if you plan on being a computer science major, are the cheaper alternatives. There are many coding boot camps out there. These camps are often significantly cheaper and shorter than college, as some only last a few months. These boot camps are designed to teach you only the knowledge required for your career, unlike college, which often requires many classes not directly relevant to your career. In addition, many offer guaranteed job placement and are backed by elite companies. Of course, do your due diligence and make sure the boot camp you select is a legitimate program. Scams do exist (for colleges, too!). It's worth noting, that even a certificate from a legitimate coding boot camp does not look as good on a resume as a four-year degree. But it should be good enough for you to land your first job as a coder. If, for some reason, you still can't get a job, use your new skills as a coder and add experience to your resume through the open-source community. For those who don't know, open-source is a term that means the underlying code to a program is accessible, free to review, and often modifiable (all computer programs, including phone apps, are built via code). Anyway, find a project (on GitHub, Bitbucket, etc.) you would enjoy working on and start coding. Or, start your own project, but ensure it is open-source and hosted online (via GitHub, Bitbucket, etc.) to give future employers the ability to review your work. In either case, make sure this new experience is prominently featured on your resume. With this additional experience and completion of a legitimate boot camp program, finding a job should not be too difficult. If it is, then the issue may be your resume or interviewing ability. These items are discussed further in Chapter 5.

Lastly, if you only want a STEM degree to earn a high income, pursuing a skilled trade, such as becoming an electrician, is a fantastic alternative. Some skilled trades can pay as much or more than many careers that require a STEM degree. Trades are truly a great way to have a fulfilling career, earn a great income to provide for your family, and avoid college. But it's worth mentioning, for those reasons, some in the media over-glorify the trades. They conveniently leave out that working in the trades can involve long hours, physically demanding labor that may cause long-term damage to the body, and exposure to harsh weather conditions. Additionally, if you believe the trades are a great way to avoid math, you would be wrong. As a matter of fact, a higher percentage of upper blue-collar workers (e.g., construction trades) perform advanced math (classified as algebra, trigonometry, statistics, and calculus) than upper white-collar workers (management, professional, technical occupations) at 41% and 35%, respectively.[6] This statistic would probably change if one were to isolate more math demanding careers such as engineering, but as someone who has worked with machinists, I can confirm they use advanced math, especially trigonometry, regularly. Regardless, if you are reading this book, you are probably hard set on earning a STEM degree. For that reason, any additional information on skilled trades is left up to the reader.

2.3. How do you decide?

Overall, I highly support college and believe it is the best path for most pursuing a STEM career. Many like to point out how flawed this path is, and they're right, it is flawed. After all, anything developed by humans is never going to be perfect. Perhaps there should be less of an emphasis on having a bachelor's degree, as we all know about the countless college drop-outs that went on to start elite companies. The fact these entrepreneurs wouldn't even be granted a job interview with their own company, had they not started it and had to apply normally, is definitely a problem. It is also concerning knowing how much talent is out there working lower-end jobs because college is not a great fit for them. However, in defense of hiring managers everywhere, you have to narrow the pool of candidates somehow. Some open positions can attract thousands of job seekers and it is unlikely that companies can (or will) provide the required time or resources to vet every candidate diligently. As a result, companies often have minimum thresholds one must meet to even be considered for an opening. For better or worse, that often means a bachelor's degree.

This requirement to go to college is only increasing in popularity too, as nearly a third of jobs that once only required a high school diploma now require a four-year degree.[7] Additionally, roughly 25% of jobs that once only required a bachelor's degree now require a master's degree. Regardless of one's opinion on the emphasis of having a bachelor's degree, there does appear to be a correlation between higher education and success. For instance, only 8% of CEOs did not complete college, 88% of millionaires graduated from college, and 84% of the 400 richest Americans have at least a bachelor's degree.[7-9] Of course, it could be argued that the success of those with a bachelor's degree is caused by a flawed system. But regardless of where someone stands on the correlation vs. causation debate, there is a clear relationship of success for those with a bachelor's degree versus those without. Therefore, it is highly recommended to pursue (and earn) a bachelor's degree, as it provides the best path for a rewarding career in STEM.

Moreover, for those who fear getting a STEM degree is too hard, and you think you'll fail, remember that "Nothing in life is more expensive than fear." Throughout history, fear has cost too many people, including people you love, a fortune. Not just financially, but emotionally and spiritually as well, because you will always be left wondering what if. Furthermore, if you're thoughtful about your approach, there are ways to mitigate risk. For example, if you fear you're not smart enough to earn a STEM degree – which is complete malarkey, by the way – then don't start your college education as a full-time student. Perhaps take one class, online or at a community college, and work hard to prove to yourself that you can earn good grades. Then add additional classes in subsequent semesters until you feel comfortable enough to tackle the load of a full-time student.

Finally, regardless of where your journey takes you, STOP talking yourself out of success. STOP letting other people talk you out of success. STOP coming up with reasons why you can't/won't succeed. STOP justifying taking the easy way out. STOP letting fear control and dictate your life. START doing! START trying, and probably failing, and trying again until you succeed! Because taking a path with no risks should never be an option as that path will almost certainly lead to a life of poverty (financially, emotionally, and spiritually).

2. Is college right for you?

2. Is college right for you?

Chapter Bullet Points

- College is the recommended path for those interested in STEM

- College is NOT right for everyone

- Give your passions and ideas a shot

- A high percentage of successful people have a bachelor's degree

- A life without risk, often leads to a life without success

Notes

_____

_____

_____

_____

_____

_____

_____

3. Methods to minimize educational costs

If college is the path you select, it is important to recognize that college is expensive, which is why educational costs are intentionally discussed early in this book. The fact I had to pay $300 a year to park my car seems insane. How is parking not covered in the already outrageous tuition and other fees students are required to pay (e.g., sustainability fee, student assessment fee, or enrollment fee)? These costs are only increasing, too. College students today pay far more than their parents and grandparents did. From 1980 to 2019–2020, college costs have increased over 180%.[10] And yes, that is accounting for inflation! Admittedly, that doesn't seem fair and it probably isn't. But that's life, and if you want a bachelor's degree, these costs must be paid somehow. The keyword being somehow, as there are numerous avenues for individuals to vastly reduce their educational costs.

I was lucky when I started college, as I had no one to lean on for advice. No one ever told me about the FAFSA (Free Application for Federal Student Aid) and how easy it is to receive money to "help" me attend college. Therefore, I had to pay out of pocket early on in my college career. Not easy for a kid stocking groceries, but I saved and went to a community college first. Admittedly, one year I did need additional help and received a small loan from my dad for a little over $900, which I repaid as soon as possible. Unfortunately, later I learned about the FAFSA and started taking out loans. Like most young adults, I took out more in loans than I really needed. The student loan industry is highly flawed, and it is far too easy for young adults to cause long-term damage to their financial health. Most, including myself, justified taking out extra loans because how much money we "would" be making in the future. Thankfully, today I am in a great place financially because I have always been frugal and, out of sheer luck, came across Dave Ramsey (the anti-debt guy). However, I can definitely see how easy it is to take out $100,000 or more in student loan debt. This ability to easily take out large sums in student loans is truly a tragedy, as it harms those who need it most: students from low-income families. Often, through no fault of their own, young adults from low-income households are less educated with regard to finances and lack a solid adviser. Unfortunately, the ones they lean on to help make sound financial decisions are ill-equipped to do so. I mean, you don't know what you don't know, and many don't even know they're making a mistake until it is too late. All they hear their whole life is how college debt is "good" debt, and how much money they'll make after college. The bottom line is that America's student loan system is broken. It sets some people up for failure by allowing literal teens – who are uneducated and lack financial experience – to take out massive loans. Making matters worse is the fact that household finance is often either not taught or only briefly skimmed in American high schools. This all leads to financial stress that causes such long-term mental health issues that one in fourteen borrowers have suicidal thoughts.[11] An even worse statistic: one in eleven suicides of young professionals is related to student loans.[12] People are literally committing suicide because of a mistake they made at 18 years old; that is a serious problem.

I apologize for the disturbing facts on suicide. However, I would have been doing you a disservice if I avoided the subject. Student loans are a serious issue, and they do create long-term stress that no one should take lightly. To help avoid this stress, one should never be in the habit of calling debt "good." Debt may be useful, such as when purchasing a home, but owing someone money you don't have is never "good." Therefore, this chapter will not provide guidance for taking on debt. It will, however, discuss methods for reducing educational costs, since that is always beneficial, regardless of how you pay.

3.1. Community college

The easiest way to reduce the cost of college is simple: go to a more cost-effective college. The average cost of college as of May 2024 is $38,270 per year per student in the United States.[13] The first tip to minimize this cost is to take advantage of in-state tuition since out-of-state tuition is roughly triple the average annual cost ($9,750 versus $28,386). But even in-state tuition is absurd compared to the average annual cost of in-district tuition plus fees to attend a community college at just $4,110, as of October 2023.[14] It's worth noting that these are averages across the United States, and depending on your region, these values may seem high or low.

There are several other factors that can impact your college costs, such as family income. This is especially true for some private colleges where the cost of education is often heavily subsidized, requiring many students to pay far less than the rate seen online. To help approximate your real cost to attend a particular college, use a net price calculator. To do this, use your favorite search engine and type in "NAME OF COLLEGE net price calculator." This should work for most colleges, from elite schools to community colleges. Of course, not all net price calculators are the same, and I would guess their accuracies vary as well. But they should give you a more accurate number to work with; though, be aware that they do ask for your parents' financial information.

If you're like many, and your net college costs appear unreachable without accumulating a significant amount of debt, then selecting a more cost-effective college is probably your best option, as it can save you tens of thousands of dollars. Fortunately, there are an abundance of cost-effective community colleges across the United States. You probably have one within driving distance. If not, remote classes may be an option. That way, like I did, you can live at home while attending community college. Depending on what your parents dictate, this may allow you to save on rent, food, electric, and other expenses, in addition to tuition. These cost savings are simply too substantial to not take advantage of, so if able, I do believe it's wise to put off your independence a few more years. Trust me, I do understand that freedom can be pretty freakin' sweet. But in most cases, it is foolish to use that as an excuse to not take full advantage of a community college and living at home. Future you will thank you endlessly for putting up with your parents for another couple of years. Remember, in the long term, when your peers are paying their ridiculously high student loan payments, you'll be using your income to save for a down payment on a house and to invest for retirement! The cost of college is NOT just the upfront cost. The debt can/will set you back and severely limit your long-term financial success.

For some reason, there is a stigma associated with community colleges, even though they often provide the same education and cover the same material as other colleges, regularly using the same textbooks as four-year universities. This is why employers tend to focus on what degree you earned, not where it was earned, and definitely not where your post-high school path started. With that in mind, I'm not necessarily suggesting you should earn a bachelor's degree from a community college. You certainly can, if it's an option for your major. But for many, local community colleges don't offer a bachelor's degree in their field. In that case, one option is to complete your basics, introductory and fundamental classes, at a community college. This normally entails spending your first two college years at a community college then transferring to a four-year university.

This does require some pre-work as your desired four-year university may not allow transfer credits, may have a limit on the number of credits that can transfer in, may only allow transfer credits from certain schools, or may have other stipulations, so do your due diligence here to avoid wasting time and money at a community college. This usually involves reviewing the website of your desired four-year university and then being in constant communication with advisers from both schools. Moreover, make sure the advisers you are communicating with are advisers for your desired major as differences in requirements do exist between departments, even at the same school. Furthermore, ask the advisers about any transfer programs for your major between the two schools. This means the community college has a list of classes that should transfer into your desired four-year university without issue, provided you pass the classes. Essentially, be proactive upfront to ensure a smooth transition between colleges, and avoid wasting time and money on non-transferable classes.

If you prefer not to start out at a community college, you may still be able to take one or two classes a semester from one while attending a four-year university. But, in addition to the previously discussed transfer limitations, there may be other reasons this is not a viable option, such as pay structure. For example, some colleges may have a flat-rate price once you hit a certain number of credits in a semester, such as 12. Thus, if you are required to be a full-time student at your desired four-year university, and they have flat-rate pricing for full-time students, it may be cheaper to just take advantage of the flat-rate pricing and add another class (or two) there instead. So, like always, do your due diligence.

But, if attending both a four-year university and a community college simultaneously makes financial sense for your situation, know that four-year universities often have local community colleges nearby. Thus, this type of situation makes it easy to enjoy the clout you might be seeking in attending a four-year university while saving you a significant amount of money by also attending a community college. Furthermore, this allows you to keep your community college experience a secret if you choose. In fact, even if you start out at a community college, long term you can still remove it from your resume. Thus, all people will ever see is a bachelor's degree in _____ from the University of _____. Though, to reiterate, I have no problem with community colleges, and I started out at one myself. In fact, many would argue that community colleges are a better fit for some people due to their smaller class sizes, especially for those first couple of years out of high school. Therefore, it is strongly encouraged to take advantage of their tremendous cost savings. Even if you only take one class per semester at a community college, and the rest at a four-year university, you can still save thousands of dollars. Of course, I would encourage fitting in more than one class per semester, but one is better than none. Also, don't forget to take advantage of summer courses, as they may provide an avenue to save on tuition, even if your four-year university has flat-rate pricing. I know there are countless other excuses for why someone can't save money by working in community college courses, and I won't try to name them all, as most are hogwash, with the exceptions being that you earned a full-ride scholarship or your university refuses to accept credits from a community college. Make sure you avoid using illegitimate excuses to justify irresponsible financial decisions.

A final perk provided by community colleges is the opportunity for a fresh start. Some of you have struggled academically and would have a hard time receiving an acceptance letter from your preferred college or any four-year university. Thankfully, community colleges exist. These colleges usually have very high acceptance rates. For some community colleges, the only real requirement is a willingness to pay tuition. If you have struggled academically, and feel unprepared for college, don't worry as community colleges typically make you take placement exams. These exams will tell your advisor what courses to place you in. If you don't do well, they'll simply place you in lower-level courses. The downside is you end up paying to retake high school-level classes that typically don't count towards a degree, but these classes will provide you with the foundation you are missing. Then, the following semester, or year, you can start taking classes that count towards a degree without being overwhelmed. The truth is, any excuse you have for why pursuing a college education is unattainable is invalid and only exists in your head. The reality is that there is always a path for you to earn a college degree. In fact, even prisons have paths for inmates to pursue a college education. The point being, if you are willing, there is an academic path for you. Your path may be dimly lit and require a lot of hard work to move all the branches and debris out of your way, but there is a path for you. It's just up to you to stop making excuses and actually start walking. One baby step at a time.

3.2. Selecting a college

Whether you choose to attend a community college or not, you'll probably finish your college career at a four-year university. Thus, I wanted to share my thoughts and experiences as selecting the right one can help improve your development and, of course, save you money. But first, I wanted to acknowledge that some of you may choose a college based on morals (e.g., your religious affiliation). I won't comment on those. I'll just repeat: always be mindful of the debt you are taking out regardless of the reason and always work hard to find ways to reduce such potential debt, such as applying for MANY scholarships.

With regard to scholarships, I know some of you have a full-ride scholarship to the school of your dreams. If that's the case, congratulations! I am proud of you, and I am glad your hard work paid off. For those of you with a partial scholarship, please do the math to ensure it's actually saving you money. I knew someone who had a half scholarship through basketball to an out-of-state school that cost over three times the amount of a normal in-state four-year university (let alone a community college). That math doesn't add up! You are still going deeper in debt than you would at a normal in-state school. Remember, you do not have to accept a partial scholarship, so do the math if you receive one. Does it actually save you money? If so, then of course accept it. If it doesn't, then simply say thanks but no thanks. Your future self will thank you for avoiding excess debt. In addition, by not taking the partial scholarship, you now have more college options. Thus, now you can select an in-state school that has a great program relative to your major. And if your partial scholarship was for sports, you can still walk-on. Who knows, as a walk-on, you may earn a scholarship at the in-state school, too. Talk about a win-win.

3.2.1. Comparing different types of colleges

There are different types of four-year universities, but I will simplify it and break them down to two types: small private schools and large public schools, as those are where my experiences lie. Starting with small private schools, one advantage is that you can have better relationships with the professors. For example, at WMU (a large public school), I was told: "You are not their [the students'] friend and don't try to be." Even though at the time, I wasn't all that much older than the students. In fact, one was older than me if I recall correctly. On the other hand, when I taught at MVNU (a small private school), I was told to be the students' friend, and that MVNU wants the students to feel like part of a community. MVNU even told me I could invite students over to my place for social events to assist in creating a welcoming environment. Another advantage of smaller schools is that it is far easier to win awards. For example, one year at MVNU we only had one electrical engineering senior, so he won the "Outstanding Electrical Engineering Senior Award" by default. So I do get why a smaller school appeals to some, but again, apply for scholarships since smaller universities tend to cost significantly more!

Outside of typically being cheaper, there are other reasons one may select a large public school. Larger schools tend to have more access to lab/research equipment, clubs and societies (This is discussed further in Section 5.3.), and more options for elective classes. Moreover, they have more options for the same class. At MVNU, Dynamics is only offered in the spring. If you fail, you cannot take it again until next spring. Most major-specific classes work that way at smaller schools. This means that if you fail, your graduation date could be set back a whole year, depending on the class. At WMU, Dynamics was offered all year long, including the summer. In addition, they often had more than one Dynamics class per semester. This variety may allow you to avoid those annoying 8:00 a.m. classes, too. Though, for most junior and senior level classes, the setup was the same as MVNU (i.e., offered once a year).

Another benefit of a larger school includes the ability to build a larger network of people who are on a similar career path. This, coupled with the fact that larger schools tend to have larger and more frequent job fairs, as well as more company tours, may help advance your career. Larger schools also have more opportunities for school pride, such as more famous alumni or ranked sport teams. For example, I was at WMU when their football team ranked #15 in the nation, which was cool to be a part of. Moreover, larger schools provide access to a wider variety of software; this includes software relevant to majors. For example, WMU had licences to use a finite element program called Abaqus. MVNU, on the other hand, had no such access and the students had to use Abaqus' learning edition, which had limitations that harm the students' learning outcome. But perhaps the best reason to choose a larger school is that you are far more likely to have an expert in that particular field teaching the class. At smaller schools, faculty can be spread thin, and they often teach classes that fall outside of their areas of expertise.

One topic that may be taboo to talk about is the grade inflation at smaller private universities. I have read about this online and seen it myself. To give examples, at WMU I was told by the former chair of the mechanical and aerospace engineering department that the average exam grade should be in the low 70s. However, when talking to a professor at MVNU (with 20+ years of teaching experience), she told me she aims for exams to be in the low 80s. To share the context, at WMU I was teaching Dynamics which is often considered a "weeder" class, and that could have played a role in why the chair told me to aim for grades in the low 70s. But that's still a drastic difference between the two schools, and that's not my only example. That same professor at MVNU told me at her previous university (a small private school), in order to give a student a final grade of C or below, they had to justify it to the other faculty within the department. Thankfully, for the latter example, that was not the case at MVNU.

Now, I just wanted to acknowledge that grades across universities are not equal; however, I'm not going to dig into whether this issue is good or bad. The reason is the issue is clearly debatable, and I can see both sides. For example, are grades higher because smaller class sizes allow students to learn better or are professors more biased since smaller class sizes allow them to know the students on a personal level? Therefore, if this is something you are interested in knowing more about, please do your own research. But regardless, with hard work, there is no reason you can't excel at any school you attend. And, if you are excelling at a smaller school, be proud, as I promise there are still plenty of students at your school who are not putting in the work and are not earning the grades you are. And, for those wondering, it has been reported that the grade inflation issue is true for private high schools as well. Though, this is out of my realm of expertise.

Finally, note that both teaching and research universities exist. At teaching universities, the professors, on average, tend to care more about teaching. This makes teaching universities a great option if your goal is to get a bachelor's degree and start working. Alternatively, research universities are a great option if you plan on conducting research, earning a master's degree with a thesis option, and/or earning a PhD. That said, either option is appropriate for your undergraduate studies.

3.2.2. Prestigious universities

I know many select a college with the expectation that selecting a higher ranked school will lead to higher career earnings, but that's not always the case. Following this paragraph are two lists: the left list ranks the top national universities (U.S. News), while the right list ranks national universities based on the mid-career pay for their alumni (payscale.com, "Bachelor's Degrees" and "All Alumni" were selected).[15, 16] Even within the top 10, these rankings are inconsistent, as no college maintains the same position and several don't even make both lists. And, as one may expect, these lists become increasingly inconsistent as the rankings get lower. So, if this is important to you, make sure you look up each college you are considering in both lists (citations are in bibliography). Though, as we will discuss in the next paragraph, selecting a college based on earning potential may not be a wise decision.

Top Universities[15]	Top Universities Based on Mid-Career Pay of Alumni[16]
1. Princeton University	1. Massachusetts Institute of Technology
2. Massachusetts Institute of Technology	2. Stanford University
3. Harvard University	3. United States Naval Academy
4. Stanford University	4. Princeton University
5. Yale University	5. Harvey Mudd College
6. University of Pennsylvania	6. Harvard University
7. California Institute of Technology	7. United States Military Academy
8. Duke University	8. Yale University
9. Brown University	9a. University of Pennsylvania
10. Johns Hopkins University	9b. Dartmouth College

If you are considering attending a prestigious university, know that they do not guarantee success, and they are not required to be successful. They can certainly help, as they provide name recognition and the opportunity to build a strong network, but you still have to put in work to succeed in life. And you can put that work in whether you went to an elite school, an in-state school, or even a community college. In fact, a study of 10,000 millionaires found that only 8% went to prestigious private schools while 62% went to public state schools.[8] But a more important fact is knowing that 88% of millionaires graduated from college. I hope that makes it clear that it does not matter where the degree is from. Rather, it's the fact you have one that greatly enhances your career path and financial success.

Pertaining to name recognition, many people believe their four-year university has name value on a resume. This often isn't the case and is nothing more than what some say to justify overspending on college. It's true that the (very few) elite colleges have name value, such as MIT, Harvard, Stanford, and Yale, but most don't attend these types of universities. And if you're not at one of the elite schools, please stop fooling yourself and thinking your school holds name value. Other than the hiring manager that went to college X, no other hiring manager will care if you went to college X or college Y. In addition, do not let school recruiters tell you otherwise. School recruiters are nothing more than sales representatives (sales reps) for the schools. Therefore, they are good at telling stories that sound true and appear to make logical sense, but remember the old wives tale about dealing with sales reps: "How do you tell if a salesman is lying? If his lips are moving." Even a good honest sales rep is going to be heavily biased; thus, be a bit of a skeptic for any information you receive from a school recruiter. Note: I am not saying don't talk to recruiters. They can absolutely have useful information, and you should talk to them. They should be able to answer your questions; though, it is always a good idea to fact check them online later to help ensure they aren't smooth talking you and trying to get you to spend more for the same education. I mean, why would you spend more for the same results? The simple answer is, you shouldn't. Think about it another way, when you selected your doctor, did you ask what college they attended? Or if you ever had surgery, did you ask your surgeon what college they attended? If you didn't, don't you think you should have? I mean, your life is in their hands! I hope you realize how silly that would be. Surgeons have qualifications they have to meet; therefore, you know you are (probably) in good hands. This is true for colleges as well. For example, ABET (the Accreditation Board for Engineering and Technology) determines the quality of engineering programs at colleges and universities. If your school is ABET-accredited, you can have faith you are in good hands. Employers know this, too, as many job postings do state the college you attend(ed) has to be ABET-accredited. However, I have yet to see a job posting that stipulates the exact college(s) you have to attend, and I have seen hundreds if not thousands of postings so far in my career.

For those who are going to a prestigious college (e.g., MIT, Stanford, or an Ivy League school), that's awesome, and I have no plans on telling you not to go. But you must do it intelligently. This means limiting student loan debt, ideally to zero. Thus, the same recommendations apply: start out at a community college, if possible, and apply for many scholarships.

3.3. Scholarships

Outside of selecting a less expensive college, the best and most productive way to reduce the cost of college is through scholarships. There is a common misunderstanding about scholarships, that they are only for "smart"/good students. It is true that there are many scholarships for students based on their past academic success; however, there are countless scholarships based on random information about you or your lifestyle. For example, I received one scholarship that is only given out to people from my hometown (and the surrounding area) and another for being born with a cleft palate/lip. These types of scholarships greatly reduce the number of applicants, thus increasing your chances of earning them. In addition, it is not unheard of for a scholarship to have too few applicants, and every one who does apply receives the scholarship.

Unfortunately, for myself, I did not really know much about scholarships until my adviser told me I needed to apply for them once my school funding ended; I had teaching and research assistantships for the first few years of graduate school. Though, I wish I knew more about scholarships as an undergraduate. For the most part, I paid for undergraduate "out of pocket" (with debt), but almost all of my graduate school was funded through a combination of school funding and scholarships. Fortunately, I received scholarships every year I applied. The trick is, don't throw all your eggs into one basket. During what I call the "scholarship application season" (December–March), you should be applying for at least 5–10 scholarships a month. Of course, you can apply for more, many more, if you can fit it into your schedule. You should also be applying outside of the "scholarship application season" and should start applying as early as the summer before your senior year of high school. The main goal is to increase your odds of earning a scholarship, or multiple scholarships. Everyone is different, and this is true for scholarship evaluators as well. This means that some will like your story, writing style, and ideas, while others may not. At the end of the day, the more you throw your name out there and actually apply, the greater your chances of earning a scholarship.

To put the odds in perspective, your odds are about 1-in-8 for earning a private scholarship and decrease to 1-in-500 for very competitive scholarships.[17] Thankfully, there's significantly more scholarship funding available than most realize. In fact, there is enough funding for every full-time enrolled student to receive $9,744.[17] Moreover, the number of awarded scholarships is increasing, by a reported 45% over the last decade, as of 2021.[18] Unfortunately, all this college funding isn't used: An estimated $100 million in scholarships goes unawarded every year, in large part due to a lack of applicants. Sadly, this number pales in comparison to the almost $3 billion in Pell Grants that are missed out on due to students failing to file their FAFSA (Free

Application for Federal Student Aid).[17] Thus, at the minimum, you need to be filling out the FAFSA. It is very simple to apply for and requires very little effort as the Pell Grant (the grant provided by the FAFSA) is mainly given out based on financial need and not on your ability to stand out via the application process. Note, however, the FAFSA is how most students take out student loans. Again, as discussed before, I won't comment on the use of loans other than you need to fully understand the stress they could put on you later in life.

I will also reiterate that under absolutely no circumstances should you justify taking out more loans than you need today based on money you'll be theoretically making tomorrow. They make it far too easy for college students to do this, but don't fall into that trap and don't justify unnecessary purchases, such as a new computer. Often, your old computer will work just fine; if not, colleges typically have computer labs. If you want a new computer (or anything else), get a job, save up, and pay cash. I'm not against buying new things, just don't use student loans to do it. Your future self will thank you. Worse yet, definitely don't use school loans to buy random items such as a bike or a gun. Unfortunately, I have seen people buy both with student loans. I would bet, if you asked a random sample of 100 former college students if they regretted taking out more student loans than the absolute minimum they needed, more often than not, you would get 100 yeses.

It's also worth knowing that scholarships can often be compounded. Since this isn't always the case, you'll need to check the rules and limitations of each scholarship you receive. But this compounding effect can make smaller scholarships more appealing, as they are typically easier to earn and can add up quickly. In fact, you may accumulate enough scholarship funding to have excess. If that is the case, your college will generally send you a refund for the difference. At this point, you need to verify the stipulations of your scholarships as some scholarships may require you to give the money back, some will allow you to spend it on other educational expenses (e.g., books, parking, a computer, housing, or summer classes), and some will just let you keep it with no strings attached. Therefore yes, in essence you can get paid to go to college. Beware though, in most cases you will have to pay taxes on the refund, and schools do not take taxes out beforehand. So, look up how much you'll owe, then set that aside until tax season.

If your scholarships don't add up to cover the cost of being a full-time student, remember being a part-time student for a semester (or longer) may be a possibility. Though there are three important factors to know: some scholarships require you to be a full-time student; the same applies for some co-op opportunities; and if you are covered by your parents' health insurance, the health insurance company (and/or the government) may require you to be a full-time student. Note that laws governing health insurance and health insurance policies do change over time. So, make sure you do your due diligence before dropping below full-time status. Regardless, with all that said, if your situation allows, don't be afraid to drop below full-time status. During the 2019–2020 school year I dropped to half-time status due to not having enough scholarship funding to cover a full-time course load. I have no regrets. It allowed me to start working full-time, giving me a head start on my long-term career. Note, my situation is probably different than yours as I already had a bachelor's degree, making it easier for me to start working on my career instead of just another job. Nevertheless, that just means you have to be more creative than me. Perhaps use the extra time to try out a business idea you have. And to be clear, I'm not saying drop to part-time for your whole college career (unless that's the only option you have for your situation). That would add more years than you probably want, and may cause you to give up on your education. Nonetheless, dropping down for a semester or two would have little to no impact on your long-term success. And if it helps reduce your student debt or stops you from accumulating any debt, I think it's an option worth exploring.

Another tip is to not hesitate to email questions to scholarship providers. Remember that rules are made by humans, and if humans want, rules can be adjusted by humans. By this I mean, if the scholarship states it needs to be used for X, you never know, they may approve the funding to be used for Y. For instance, for one of my scholarships, the plan was to take two summer classes; however, I did not receive enough scholarship funding to fully cover the cost of those classes, so I asked if that stipulation could be waived. This was their reply: "Hi Justin, that is fine. The scholarship was already paid to your school with a letter to use it in the way that best helps you. So you can have them apply it to the fall, if you like."

As far as finding scholarships, professors are a great resource, as they consistently help members of their research team apply for them. They'll have ideas you have never thought of nor would ever come across via a web search. Moreover, if they know you and you're a good student, they may have an inside scoop on a scholarship and may offer to help you earn it.

Outside of professors, typically finding scholarships involves a lot of web searching. A few standard places to look include professional societies, college websites, and government websites. Professional societies often have scholarship opportunities posted online, so at least review the societies related to your areas of interest/field (e.g., American Society of Mechanical Engineers, American Institute of

Aeronautics and Astronautics, or SAE International). With regard to college websites, colleges often post scholarship opportunities online. Don't limit your search to just your college either, as many of these opportunities have nothing to do with the college you are attending. Meaning, there is no reason you can't apply for scholarships posted on other colleges websites. The University of Michigan and the University of California, Berkeley, are great resources in this regard. Finally, government websites, such as NASA or the Department of Defense, are fantastic resources as well. Often their scholarships can be highly competitive, but they can be highly lucrative, too.

The resources just listed should be utilized before random web searches, as scholarship opportunities from professors, professional societies, college websites, or government websites are probably legitimate. Unfortunately, many of the generic scholarship websites on the open web are nothing more than data mining sites. Even many that are legitimate, can often have lower standards with regard to vetting scholarships. I don't say this to discourage you, but just to remind you it's something to be mindful of. Applying for scholarships can be time-consuming, thus I don't want you to waste time on data mining sites.

One last thing that is important to remember about finding scholarships is the fact you are unique. Use that to your advantage. Your uniqueness will make you eligible for scholarships many can't apply for. For example, I received a $500 scholarship for being born with a cleft lip and palate from the American Cleft Palate-Craniofacial Association. (Thank You!) I have also received thousands from the Grand Traverse Regional Community Foundation. (Thank You!) Their scholarships are only offered to students from Traverse City and the surrounding area. Since these scholarships aren't offered to the world, I had to compete against a much smaller pool of applicants. Thus, when you start looking for scholarships, don't forget to look for scholarships related to your uniqueness, too. Are you a minority? Did you grow up in poverty? Are you handicapped? You really need to ask yourself, What is different about me? Even if it's a negative, why not turn a negative into a positive, such as being born with a cleft lip and palate?

3.3.1. General scholarship information

Scholarship deadlines are typically between December–March for the following school year. (For example, a deadline between December 2019 and March 2020 would provide funding for Fall 2020/Spring 2021.) A good approach is to start looking for scholarships roughly a year in advance. For example, if your fall semester starts in September, you should start looking into scholarships in October/November of the prior year. This will give you time to figure out what scholarships you want to apply to, the work required for those scholarships, and what order to apply in. This will help you avoid missing any due dates. Obviously, scholarships due in December should be higher on the priority list than those due in March. As an aside, note that funding is usually split between the fall and spring semesters. (For example, if you receive $1,000 in scholarship funding, you would receive $500 in the fall and another $500 in the spring.)

Scholarship applications typically require one or two letters of recommendation. Therefore, it's beneficial to identify and contact two to three people early that are willing to write you a strong letter of recommendation. When contacting them, it's important to phrase your language in question form. In other words, don't tell them they're writing you a letter of recommendation; ask them if they're willing to. Also, if they are willing to, let them know that no letter of recommendation is required as of now, but that you plan on applying for scholarships over the next couple of months.

When identifying people to contact, keep in mind that who writes your letters of recommendation is important. Letters from family and friends often hold little weight in the eyes of evaluators, so try to avoid using them. A former manager would be a better option; for some, this may be your only option. However, the best option is to have former and/or current teachers and professors write your letters of recommendation. These scholarships are for school; therefore, someone who can validate your work ethic related to school will hold the most weight. A solid letter from a teacher will look better than the world's greatest letter of recommendation from a family member. In addition, teachers and professors have more experience in writing letters of recommendation. They will have a better understanding of what evaluators are looking for, and can tailor your letter accordingly.

In addition to letters of recommendation, some scholarship applications require a personal narrative. Be aware that writing a good one will be time-consuming. Remember that you are competing against others for college funding, even when applying for low-end scholarships, so you need a personal narrative that stands out. Writing this will take hours upon hours, but it isn't as bad as it sounds, as once you do it, you can use large portions from your first personal narrative on future personal narratives. Thus, once your first personal narrative is complete, simply create and edit a copy of it for each new scholarship. This is done by adding and highlighting (figuratively) important details while removing information that is not relevant to the scholarship you are currently applying for.

As far as what information to include in a personal narrative, that is dependent on the scholarship you are applying for. The scholarship itself should have guidelines to follow. But you should also be asking yourself what is the scholarship trying to support and promote. For example, I earned a scholarship for doctoral students who were pursuing a career as a college professor. For that scholarship, my personal narrative focused on outlining the path I plan on following to achieve a career as a professor; what I plan on doing within that career (e.g., what type of research); what experiences I had that motivated my aspirations to pursue a career as a professor; and what experiences I've had that would contribute to my ability to become an excellent professor.

To write an excellent personal narrative, you simply have to start. Your first draft probably won't be very good, and that's perfectly fine. Even if you believe it's great and it would have earned you an A in high school, it's still best to be humble. Remember, you are now competing against a much larger pool of students, and all these students are equally as talented as you. Thus, one attempt isn't good enough. With this in mind, here are some steps to help you write an excellent personal narrative.

1. Write a multi-page personal narrative

2. Allow time to pass before editing, then when editing, be proactive and focus on:

   a) Removing low-quality content

   b) Adding more high-quality content

   c) Removing blockingness

   d) Improving your word selection

3. Edit again, but this time use a text-to-speech reader

4. If you are able to, receive feedback from someone with experience

5. Edit your paper based off the feedback you received

6. After final edit, run the paper through a text-to-speech program one more time

7. Good news, you're "done"

There is no right or wrong with regard to how long your first draft should be. I only say "multi-page" to imply it needs to be longer than one page (which is the typical required length). The point is, the first draft should be longer than your final draft. There is always fluff to be removed. If you normally write a lot of fluff to meet page count limits, you'll probably have to cut out more than most. Thus, your first draft should be longer than most (perhaps over three pages). And if you're an exceptional writer, and actually take time to write the first draft well, you can get away with writing less. Although, remember that a longer draft is preferable, as you will be removing the excess length later. Ultimately, just be honest with yourself, and as always, be your own worst critic.

Furthermore, when you start writing make sure to use examples. Don't just say you're a great student, but include examples of how you're a great student. I know it can be awkward talking about your successes, at least it was for me. Nevertheless, scholarship evaluators do not know you, and they can't take you at your word, nor should they. They need evidence to support your claims. In addition, words such as good or great are arbitrary, and arbitrary words like those don't really mean anything. One person's great is another person's average. It's your examples of past success, and not your opinion of yourself, that truly sets you apart from other applicants. Each of the following examples includes a statement from a writer giving an opinion of themselves (writer "a") versus a writer supporting their claims with evidence (writer "b"). Which writer do you believe more?

1. Example #1:

   a) I'm a great student and a hard worker.

   b) I have a proven track record of hard work, as I maintain a 3.7 GPA while working part-time and playing high school football.

2. Example #2:

   a) I'm a fantastic leader.

   b) Due to exhibiting fantastic leadership abilities, I was voted captain of my high school debate team.

3. Example #3:

   a) I like to give back to my community.

   b) I understand the importance of giving back; thus I regularly donate my time to _____.

After your first draft is complete, wait at least a week (if time allows) and then edit. This waiting period allows you to catch mistakes you simply wouldn't catch without a break from writing. To assist even further, read the paper out loud during this editing step. This combination – of both waiting and reading out loud – does wonders with assisting you in finding grammatical errors. This is also a good time to cut the paper down by removing all the low-quality content (i.e., fluff). Though, if (when) during that waiting period you are able to think of more high-quality content, never be afraid to add it in.

While editing, don't forget to remove blockingness from your writing either, as papers should have a nice flow when reading. (Blockingness refers to a lack of natural flow between sentences, resulting in an abrupt stop and start that you can almost feel as you read.) One way to do this is using transition words and phrases. A simple web search will help you find good transitions (e.g., thus, therefore, regardless, furthermore, or equally important). Additionally, thesauruses can be helpful tools for this and are one of the best tools a writer can use, as they also help you avoid using a word repetitively while improving your word selection (e.g., replace "great" with "remarkable" or replace "found everywhere" with "ubiquitous"). More information on how to eliminate blockingness, transition words, and thesauruses can be reviewed in Chapter 7.

Next, to help illustrate the importance of word selection and a proper writing flow, are a few examples comparing different versions of (roughly) the same sentence. It should be clear which version is better (with "b" being the improved sentence) and how constructing sentences slightly differently can significantly increase the reader's perception of the writer's intelligence.

1. Example #1:

   a) My goal is to get a PhD from _____. This goal will help me reach my ultimate career goal of becoming a professor.

   b) Earning a PhD from _____ would provide me with the required tools and qualifications to become a professor.

2. Example #2:

   a) I would like to specialize in structural mechanics and use tools such as Finite Element Analysis (FEA) and Discrete Element Methods (DEM).

b) While I pursue a PhD, I plan on specializing in structural mechanics and developing expertise in the techniques known as Finite Element Analysis (FEA) and Discrete Element Methods (DEM).

3. Example #3:

   a) They are useful tools used in industry, and when combined, they could be used to solve more complicated problems.

   b) They are both powerful tools, and coupled together could provide a path to solving complex problems.

4. Example #4:

   a) My research is attempting to understand how cleats and turf interact via DEM; DEM used in this fashion has not been done previously.

   b) Due to a gap in existing literature, this research will examine the mechanics between synthetic surfaces and studded footwear via DEM.

5. Example #5:

   a) I have a long history of being a great leader.

   b) I have an extensive background that clearly demonstrates my leadership abilities, such as _____.

The next step in the editing process involves using a text-to-speech reader. These readers can be found for free online. Unfortunately, they are free since they are often data collection tools. While this may not concern most, it is something to be aware of. But the benefit of using them is that they allow your writing to be read aloud to you. This will help you find additional mistakes, such as awkward sentences or the use of incorrect words, as it's far too common to read what you meant to say, and not what you actually wrote. Fortunately, text-to-speech readers don't make assumptions nor fill in missing words as the human brain is known to do. This advantage is why I suggest using a text-to-speech reader over having a friend or family read it to you. Plus, it saves you from the awkwardness of making such a request and is considerate of other people's time. As far as how to implement text-to-speech readers, that's up to you. For me, depending on where I'm at in the editing process or how I feel about the writing, I either copy and paste one paragraph or one sentence into them at a time.

Nevertheless, it's still important to receive feedback from another human. Often, your friends and family are poor choices. Ideally, you want someone with experience in writing for grants and scholarships, such as a professor, as they will have significantly better insight. Warning: Feedback from a professor often calls for a large amount of rewriting and editing, which is fantastic as your paper will be significantly better for it. But obviously, redoing all that work won't feel so fantastic in the moment. If receiving feedback from a professor isn't an option, remember any feedback is better than none. However, if you do rely on friends or family, be selective. Try to find someone with a skill set that would be beneficial. For example, don't just use your dad because he's your best friend. Instead, consider asking that aunt you barely know who just so happens to be an English teacher. Moreover, feel free to receive feedback from more than one person. Though, for a personal narrative, avoid asking more than one professor. This is because some consider it rude to use up the time of several professors, as they have many students that need assistance with various tasks. Alternatively, your friends and family will probably only have one person asking for help: you.

Once you're finished editing based on the feedback you received, reread it out loud and/or run it through a text-to-speech reader one last time. This will help you catch any errors you may have just created. Now, the good news, you're finally "done." While it can always be improved further, at this stage, your personal narrative should at least be competitive. Note: It can be fun to compare your first draft to your final. Hopefully, it's blatantly clear why the first draft required so much work.

Note that if after editing your personal narrative, it still exceeds the maximum length requirement for the scholarship you are applying for, then start removing the least relevant information. It is a common misconception that more is better. This simply isn't true; often less is more. Remember that evaluators have numerous submissions to review, not just yours. They don't want to read more than what is required, and they definitely don't want to read fluff, irrelevant information, ramblings, or even unnecessary words. Avoid saying something in ten words that can be said in five. Additionally, I understand that some of you have an extensive list of accomplishments and feel, in your case, that it is acceptable to exceed the maximum length requirement. My counterargument is that if you genuinely have accomplished a lot, the best of your accomplishments should still set you apart from the crowd. In summary, if the scholarship wants you to submit a one-page personal narrative, submit a one-page personal narrative!

3.4. Open-source

Because required software for college can exceed thousands of dollars, eliminating or reducing these costs is another avenue for minimizing college expenses. Typically, college related software has student versions, and these versions are a great choice for reducing expenses. While student versions often lack the full array of features the software has to offer, they usually have essential features required for school and often cost only between $100 and $200 dollars. Sometimes, they're even free. (Note that to access student versions of software, often an active college email address is required.)

Another viable option for eliminating software costs is to utilize open-source software, as most proprietary software has a free open-source alternative. (Note that not all open-source software is free.) For those unfamiliar, open-source simply means the source code is *open* (viewable) to the public. Next, to assist in your exploration of the open-source world, we will discuss a few examples of proprietary software and their open-source counterparts.

Applications within the Microsoft Office suite are perhaps the most widely used software programs in college, especially Word and PowerPoint. Since a wide array of colleges provide Microsoft Office programs for free to their students, it is advised for most to take advantage of the free access. This is because these programs are extremely feature-rich and are significantly more common in a professional setting. Though one drawback is that after graduation, you'll lose free access to these programs (except at work). This means you'll either have to purchase Microsoft Office or use alternative programs to open the files you created in college. While the latter is a fine option, the format of files when transitioning programs is often degraded and reformatting can be time-consuming.

If you don't have free access or you're among the minority that actually plans on reviewing or reusing school files after graduation, then it may be worth it to just avoid Microsoft Office. To achieve this, two of the better Microsoft Office alternatives are Google Workspace and LibreOffice. They may not be as feature-rich as Microsoft Office, but they are feature-rich in their own right and, in my experience, completely capable of handling any required task. Based on my observations, Google applications are the primary replacement for Microsoft Office. Nevertheless I have used LibreOffice for years, including for some of my PhD work, and believe it is a fantastic open-source option. As a closing suggestion, FreeOffice appears to be worth exploring, although I have not used it, yet.

Next, it's important to discuss programming, as it's a common task for STEM students. While there are a plethora of open-source solutions, MATLAB, which is proprietary, is still prominent, at least within engineering. There are several reasons for its widespread use. It's easy to learn, has immense capabilities, has a long and established track record, and people are resistant to change, especially once a skill is developed. However, even the student edition costs money (at least as of 2024). Thankfully, there are free alternatives, such as Octave and Python. Octave is the more direct replacement, and a high percentage of code developed in MATLAB will execute natively in Octave and vice versa. Additionally, both MATLAB and Octave use the same file extension (.m). As a result, if your class requires MATLAB, Octave may be your best option. That said, if you're willing to self-educate, which is a highly valuable skill, then Python is worth exploring. Your professor may be unwilling or unable to assist if you choose this route, but it's not as daunting as it may appear, as Python is well documented and has a large community. (Don't forget to ask for your professor's approval before using an alternative language.)

Fortunately, schools are shifting towards Python. In fact, since 2014, the most popular programming language for introductory computer science courses is Python.[19] A justification for this trend is that Python is commonly ranked as the top programming language to learn.[20, 21] My path through college went as follows: MATLAB → Octave → Python (with other languages thrown in there for fun, e.g., C++, Julia, and Fortran). Truth be told, I don't foresee myself leaving Python any time soon. Python is incredibly feature-rich, and not just for engineering students, as it is commonly employed for website development, data science, graphical user interface (GUI) creation, robotics, etc. There's even an old quote to support Python's comprehensive capabilities: "Python isn't the best language for anything; however, it is the second-best language for everything." While I am not here to confirm or deny that, just know that Python does often rank as one of the most popular programming languages.[22-24] Note: If you choose Python and use Windows, look into Anaconda (just do a web search for "python anaconda").

As a disclaimer, there are valid situations where Python should not be implemented, such as programming real-time control systems for autonomous vehicles. Python could be utilized for prototyping ideas or for non-time-critical applications, such as the touchscreen. However, for programming time-critical applications, such as collision avoidance, programming languages such as C/C++ would be the superior choice. This is because the execution speed of C/C++ is significantly faster than Python. Since this is the case, you may be wondering why C/C++ isn't universally employed, and that's because C/C++ is far more complex than Python. In programming, there are two common speeds to evaluate: execution speed and development speed. And Python's development speed is significantly faster than that of C/C++. In layman's terms, far less technology would exist if we implemented C/C++ universally.

In addition to programming, a subset of STEM majors are also tasked with learning computer-aided design (CAD). Free access to the prominent CAD programs used within industry is typically provided by your college, often within the school's computer lab. Additionally, while enrolled as a student, you may be able to install and use these programs on your own computer for free. If not, or if you prefer to avoid long-term licensing issues upon graduation, know that open-source CAD programs exist as well. A popular one for 3D modeling is FreeCAD, which I have used regularly for school, personal, and small industry projects.

However, if you choose to use a proprietary option, it would be wise to research what CAD program is prominent in your career field and use that one, if you're able to. There are a few ways to discover which CAD program is prominent in your field. You could perform a simple web search or ask your professors. You could also find careers relative to your future goals and see what CAD programs they list on their current job postings. The reason for this research is that using the "wrong" CAD program can decrease your chances of advancing past the human resources (HR) interview step during the interview process, as HR often seems uninformed that switching between CAD programs is common practice. They tend to only count CAD experience if the experience is within the CAD program their company uses. That said, if you do choose the "wrong" program or an open-source option, then utilize your school's free access to use the "right" CAD program listed on the job posting prior to the interview or even prior to applying. The goal here is to ensure you can, honestly, include the "right" CAD program on your resume and to be able to discuss a model you designed using the "right"

CAD program during the HR interview step, so don't worry about modeling anything too complex.

At this point, you may be wondering why I recommended using the "right" software for CAD, at least before the interview, but not for Microsoft Office or programming. Well, with regard to Microsoft Office, it is considered an assumed skill, and I doubt you'll ever be tested on or even asked about your Microsoft Office capabilities. In addition, the learning curve for Microsoft Office is low as Microsoft does a fantastic job in making their software user-friendly. For the latter, the time commitment to learn another programming language right before an interview is probably too severe, especially for those early in their programming careers. But with that said, Python is heavily used in industry, and I would argue having Python as a skill makes you more marketable than most, if not all, other programming languages, including proprietary ones.

Finally, I did want to briefly address the stigma associated with open-source software for being unsafe or unreliable. This stigma is unwarranted and often caused by proprietary software companies attempts to increase sales, which can be hypocritical, as proprietary software is regularly built using open-source code. In fact, the majority, if not all, of the technology you own was built using open-source code. Furthermore, companies don't just use open-source for nonessential tasks, either. A 2015 survey revealed that 78% of companies around the world used open-source software for vital operations.[25] Thus, if companies trust open-source code for their vital operations, then I think we can agree that open-source is safe and reliable enough for your homework.

If you're still hesitant, then I encourage you to test out open-source software for yourself. It's usually free, so time would be your only cost. In doing so, you'll likely discover that open-source software is feature-rich, fully capable of scholarly work, and a fantastic alternative to proprietary software.[26-28] The only real potential negatives associated with open-source software can be its ease of use and its array of features relative to proprietary software. With regard to both, it's a software-by-software basis on whether or not these issues actually exist or if they would actually affect your use cases.

3.5. Other miscellaneous methods

Negotiating provides another avenue for reducing college costs. Unfortunately, I did not use this method, as I did not know you could. Since I don't have personal experience with this type of negotiating, you should take my advice here with a grain of salt and seek additional resources for more information. That said, here's some preliminary information to get you started. First, not all schools will negotiate, and like in all negotiations, you cannot have your heart set on anything. Once you fall in love, you'll probably overpay. Thus, be willing to save money by going to a different school. Next, calculate the total cost (tuition, room and board, food, etc.) from several colleges that are comparable to your preferred college (net price calculators and college ranking websites are advantageous here), and then create a list of those that are less expensive. Email that list to your preferred college and ask if they are willing to lower their costs to be competitive with the colleges on your list. Depending on the college, they may say no or be willing to negotiate. But without asking, you'll never know. Of course, the caveat is your preferred college must view the other colleges on your list as equivalent or superior. Harvard probably won't lower their costs to match those of a community college. Therefore, if you plan on going to a public state school, find the cheapest public state schools in that state, and use those as your bargaining chip. Similarly, you can do the same for private schools.

For those willing, military service provides a fantastic way to subsidize your college costs. Since I did not use this approach either, my knowledge on this subject is also limited. That said, I do know the government pays a large portion of college expenses for those who serve. In some cases, they completely pay for college and pay you a stipend for attending. The military even has special programs for those in college, such as the Reserve Officers' Training Corps (ROTC) or College Student Pre-Commissioning Initiative (CSPI). That's about all I know, but if joining the military has ever crossed your mind, I strongly believe it is worth your time and effort to investigate their opportunities more thoroughly.

In the pursuit of cutting costs wherever possible, one good strategy is to hold off on purchasing "required" materials for your classes, at least until you have verified they are actually required. For example, many engineering professors list engineering paper as a "required" material but very few actually require it. For those who don't know, engineering paper can be upwards of twenty times the cost of normal notebook paper. So once I learned it wasn't actually "required," I stopped using it, except for those rare classes where the professor would deduct points for not using the "correct" paper.

Perhaps an even better example would be the "required" textbooks. In order to confirm what textbooks were necessary, I knew some students who waited until after the first day of class to purchase them. This approach is dangerous, however, as professors can assign homework on the first day. Thus, forcing you to purchase textbooks at the school's overpriced bookstore instead of online. If you do use this approach, confirm that you have friends who have purchased the textbooks beforehand, so you have immediate access if needed. Of course, you could also email your professors before the semester begins to ask if their listed textbook is required and if so, whether the listed edition is necessary. Often, professors will list the newest edition of the textbook on the syllabus, even though they are fine with you using an older edition. Depending on the textbook, the older edition can be a fraction of the cost and have almost identical content. Frequently, new editions only have minor updates, such as fixed typos and updated problem sets. Updated problem sets may cause your professor to require that you at least have access to the newest edition, as they may use problems from the book for homework. (Note that access can usually be achieved via a friend's copy.) Alternatively, you could also rent a PDF copy of your required textbooks. This option is usually much cheaper than buying or renting a hard copy.

Lastly, prior to starting college, take time and investigate options to test into more advanced classes. Typically, this is accomplished with your ACT or SAT scores. If you do well on either, you can normally bypass a handful of remedial and/or freshman-level classes. This could save you thousands, if not tens of thousands, of dollars. So, take these exams seriously and study beforehand! (Ample resources for studying can be found online, including free ones.) If you fail to do well the first time, note that you can take these exams more than once to improve your score. Aside from the ACT or SAT, your school may have alternative options for bypassing remedial and/or freshman-level classes. For example, MVNU allowed students to take the ALEKS exam, and if they did well (again, don't forget to study beforehand), they could bypass math classes through precalculus. The ALEKS exam takes 60–90 minutes, and as of 2024, it was $20 versus precalculus which is a semester long and can cost up to $1,000 or more, depending on the school. That difference alone justifies

3. Methods to minimize educational costs

taking the ALEKS exam, even without factoring in the classes you would be bypassing that precede precalculus. In summary, consult your college advisor about course bypass options available to you.

Chapter Bullet Points

- Student loans can be dangerous

- Community colleges provide an incredible path to reducing college expenses

- Small scholarships add up quickly

- Top resources for scholarships: professors, professional societies, college websites, and government websites

- Student versions and open-source options can reduce software expenses

- Options exist to test out of remedial and/or freshman-level classes

Notes

_____

_____

_____

_____

4. Selecting a major

Now that we've discussed whether college is necessary and ways to reduce educational expenses, it's time discuss methods for selecting a major. For some of you, this is fairly easy. You're passionate about something, and nothing I say will change your goals. And that's great! However, there are countless others for whom picking a major is an incredibly difficult decision. In their minds, this choice will dictate their career for the rest of their lives. Thus, I would like to start by easing some pressure off of this decision, as it does not have to dictate your career path. To be frank, you don't even have to pursue a career relative to your major. In industry, you'll find countless people employed in fields unrelated to their degree. In fact, only 27% of college graduates have a career that is closely related to their major.[29]

Admittedly, those working in jobs unrelated to their major may be doing so against their wishes. I won't comment too much on working a job you don't enjoy, or worse, working a job you hate, since that is not the focal point of this book. However, I will point out that it is your choice to stay in a career you hate. Every day that you wake up and you're not proactively seeking other opportunities or even new roles within the same company, you are making the choice to stay there and be miserable. Regardless of what your current HR department says about how great your situation is, just know there are endless companies out there with pay and benefits as good, or better, than your current employer. Take everything HR says with a grain of salt, and do your own research.

Moreover, if you do find yourself lacking career satisfaction, don't think you're alone as only 34% of employees are involved at work, and are enthusiastic about their work and workplace.[30] An even worse statistic is that Monday has the highest rate of heart attacks (while Saturday has the lowest).[31] The risk of a heart attack is 11% higher on Monday than other work days (Tuesday–Friday), and as much as 20% higher for younger workers. A common belief is that the increase is caused by the stress of returning to work. As a result, finding work you enjoy can literally be lifesaving. You should always be asking yourself, "What am I doing today to improve my tomorrow?" If the answer is nothing, then your tomorrow won't get better. You need to start applying for careers that are a better fit, start a side hustle, or both. This is your life, and you're in control. Stop relying on wishful thinking and luck, and start relying on action and work!

Circling back to the topic of selecting a major, please know selecting the right major can be highly beneficial. It's just not the life or death decision some students make it out to be. A college degree is a tool that helps you obtain a career in industry, and a degree in the right major can significantly enhance that tool. With a bachelor's degree in the wrong field, you'll probably have to start lower on the totem pole. This typically means less pay and performing the tedious tasks that no one else wants to do. While these pitfalls are true for most entry-level careers, they are often amplified without the correct credentials (e.g., a bachelor's degree in that field).

With that said, I do understand the difficulties of selecting the "right" major, as I started out as a business major. And, as also discussed in Chapter 1, I barely recall why I switched to aerospace engineering. Furthermore, if I could select a major today, it might be computer science or biomedical engineering. I hope the key take-away from my inability to select the best major for myself is simple: You need to do your research, which is something I never did before college. You don't know what you don't know, and one of the best ways to fill in gaps of knowledge is through your own research. Truth be told, before college, I didn't know that programming could be a career. In fact, I didn't even know what code was. I guess I just assumed electronics ran on black magic. You know, similar to how airplanes fly. However, even a vague search as simple as "Top STEM degrees" would have yielded plenty of results discussing computer science. Thus, you should start exploring different degrees today. There is an endless amount of content on the internet for this, including articles and videos.

In addition, if able, talk to industry professionals. Far too often, I see late teens and young adults only lean on their parents for advice, not realizing their parents are only human, meaning they don't have endless knowledge. Unless their profession aligns with your major, their advice may not be relevant, as they might give you bad information. To be clear, this is not done with malicious intent. They are simply trying to help you the best they can. Unfortunately, without actual experience, the advice from anyone can be misleading to downright awful. For this reason, it is strongly encouraged to talk to industry professionals. If you're able to, gather as much information as you can, such as:

1. What is their average day like? Week? Month?

2. What do they like about their career? What do they love?

3. What don't they like about their career? What do they hate?

4. Are they happy with their selected major? Why or why not?

5. What other majors might they select now if they could go back in time?

6. What mistakes have they made throughout their career?

7. What do they wish they knew at your age?

8. If their kids were following in their footsteps, what advice would they give them?

9. What skills don't they have but wish they had developed, and why?

10. What skills did they develop that ended up being a waste of time, and why?

Note that those who work in the same discipline, such as mechanical engineers, can have vastly different roles and job responsibilities. These differences can be so extreme, it can feel like two completely different disciplines. Therefore, as usual, embrace everything one person says tentatively. But what is exceedingly helpful are trends, hence the importance of gathering information from multiple industry professionals. For example, if you interview several mechanical engineers across different companies with differing job responsibilities and they all say they use algebra regularly, then if you choose mechanical engineering as your discipline, it should be apparent that you need to take algebra seriously.

Since most of you don't have access to a broad network of individuals in your desired discipline, know that there are ways to increase your ability to connect with professionals, such as attending hiring events. These types of events are often organized by your high school or college, and generally all are welcome to attend. At these events, companies give a presentation, often including information not easily found online. Of course, the presentations are biased and talk about how great their company is. Regardless, they still provide a wealth of information and give you the ability to connect with those working in the field.

I once attended a hiring event for a medical device company, where they were featuring their surgical power tools division. After the presentation, they let us use and test the tools and gave us a free lunch, too. Next, they divided us into small groups, with each group being led by one of their engineers. This was perhaps the most impactful part, as we had the opportunity to ask any and all questions we wanted. Times like these provide the best opportunity to ask good and tough questions, questions that actually mean something to you. For example, What is one thing you don't like about this company? What is one thing you don't like about being an engineer?

Never be afraid to ask the tough questions, as they can be the most informative. Thus, make sure to come prepared with a list of questions. Lastly, at the end of the event, they did a Q&A session with a small group of engineers to answer any additional questions. This was helpful as well, but the answers were more censored. Most people are more honest one-on-one, or even in small groups, than speaking to a crowd, especially when their bosses are within the crowd.

The best, but perhaps the hardest, method to determine if a major is a good fit is to actually do the work. For example, there is no reason potential computer science majors can't start learning to code today, as they have ample free resources available to them online. For those pursuing computer science, to get started, first do research and determine where your interests lie: website design, game development, app development, etc. Then research what programming languages are actively and extensively used in that field. Next, start working your way through online tutorials. Once you grasp the basics, think of a project you would enjoy and just do it. It will be time-consuming, progress will be slow, and you'll make a ton of mistakes. Nevertheless, you'll learn a lot, acquire real experience, and gain valuable insight on the question: "Can this major provide me with a long fulfilling career?" Even if you learn the answer is no, it was still a beneficial experience, as you can now shift your focus to other majors.

Of course, some majors are for careers where attempting to gain real-world experience on your own without a proper background is unwise. A prime example of this is marine biology, as it can be unsafe interacting with wild animals. With that said, options still exist to gain actual experience. For example, you can contact marine biologists and offer to assist them. Your chances of them accepting the offer significantly improve if you mention that you plan on pursuing a bachelor's degree in marine biology, you're willing to do grunt work, and you'll work for free. If you do pursue this route and consistently get rejected, just remember that life isn't always easy. So, be creative and resourceful to find other ways to gain hands-on experience.

For example, there are research summer camps. At MVNU, we offered week-long camps for high schoolers in a variety of majors. Of course, there are negatives to pursuing this option, such as the short duration, which can make it difficult to assess if you would enjoy performing the same activities at camp for a career (i.e., for 40+ hours a week, over a few decades). Moreover, while career options within a major are broad, these camps usually focus on one or two aspects of a discipline. For instance, our mechanical engineering part of the engineering camp focused on CAD design. While a lot of engineers do use CAD, their usage varies, and many engineers never touch CAD their whole career. So, like with anything else, avoid jumping to conclusions based on these camps. Instead, use them as an additional data point to help in your decision-making process.

With regard to college minors, in my experience, they have little to no impact. In fact, I have a minor in mathematics, and it has never been discussed during an interview. Since this may change depending on your major, please conduct your own research to determine whether they actually improve your future career prospects. For those pursuing aerospace or mechanical engineering, I strongly suggest you don't overthink it or spend too much time pursuing them. If a minor you're interested in only requires an additional class or two, then perhaps take them. Otherwise, avoid minors not built into your major's curriculum, as there is no way to justify the cost of something that has little to no ROI (return on investment). Keep in mind that ROI isn't just about money, either; it also includes time. This wasted time accumulates quickly, too. For instance, classes are usually three credits and span 15 weeks. If we use the rule of thumb that homework requires (a minimum of) 1–3 hours per credit hour per week, the time to complete one course is between 90 and 180 hours (class time plus homework time). That's a very significant amount of time for basically nothing in return. That time could have been used elsewhere to generate an actual ROI, such as boosting your GPA in other courses.

Truth be told, even if there is a minor you have a legitimate interest in, I still wouldn't recommend pursuing it, as college is too expensive. Instead, utilize other resources, such as the endless free tools available online. Or just read a book or two on the topic.

At the end of the day, just remember that life is full of tough decisions. When facing them, gather as much information as you reasonably can, and then make the best choice possible with the knowledge you have at that moment in your life. Occasionally, you will still make the wrong choice. Learn from it, correct it if possible, and move on. There is no reason to dwell on it, as it won't be your last mistake.

Chapter Bullet Points

- Talk to industry professionals

- Don't be afraid to ask tough questions

- Start working in the field of your desired major ASAP

- College minors in your discipline may offer little to no ROI

Notes

5. Why gaining experience matters and how to do it

One aspect that many college students neglect is the importance of gaining actual experience. They're overly focused on their academic performance and often forget the main reason they're even going to college, which is to increase their employability in their desired field. This chapter is designed to help you redirect some of your academic energy towards other areas that will enhance your ability to find full-time employment upon graduation.

5.1. Real-world experience

If your goal is to start your career immediately after undergrad, then gaining relevant real-world experience, such as internships, outweighs the pursuit of a high GPA. In fact, during job fairs and job interviews, every company asked about my previous relevant work experience, while only a handful asked about my GPA. This was true for my friends as well. Moreover, the importance of experience is supported by research, as the Society for Human Resource Management reviewed 95,000 job postings in 2018 and found 61% of entry-level jobs required at least three years of experience.[32]

A high GPA can be very advantageous, especially for those pursuing graduate school or a career at an elite company directly after undergrad. However, for the latter, these companies still prefer a high GPA to be coupled with relevant work experience. Hence, many who work for elite companies begin their careers at non-elite companies. And often after accumulating a few years of full-time experience, it's common for people to remove their GPA from their resume. The reason being, at this point, your performance in the working world is paramount, as companies understand that college success doesn't necessarily lead to industry results.

Elite companies valuing work experience over a high GPA isn't limited to full-time careers either. For example, a Blue Origin recruiter once told me they try to avoid hiring interns without previous internship experience; often, they won't even consider them for the role. My thought was perhaps the same as yours: "Aren't internships designed to help students gain experience?" I was dumbfounded that regardless of your GPA, school projects, or extracurricular activities, you would struggle to land an internship interview with them. Now, I suspect they wanted the high GPA and extracurricular activities too. It was just shocking that those were secondary considerations for an internship. For context, this conversation was not during an interview, and I had previous internship experience at the time.

The reason previous work experience is highly valued stems from the difficulties companies and recruiters face in trying to hire employees with strong work ethics, whom they have never worked with. This means they need to rely on other factors to determine one's work ethic, such as a high GPA. However, I have learned over the years what companies already knew, GPAs are not a measure of intelligence but actually a measure of work ethic relative to school work. While that is a useful metric, a better metric to determine a candidate's ability to deliver results in industry is, previous industry results.

Fortunately for engineering majors, as well as some of the other STEM majors, an additional benefit of gaining relevant real-world experience is the pay, as internships and co-ops are typically paid and paid well. This can be highly desirable for those living on their own. I remember my first internship paid almost double my average hourly rate as a grocery stocker; it was definitely life-altering money for someone with my background.

5.2. Academic experience

Another way to gain experience is by pursuing opportunities within academia, such as becoming a teaching assistant. This type of work can vary but typically involves grading homework, teaching labs, or both. The best part is that, depending on the professor's level of need, a high GPA isn't always required, especially if the student is willing to work for free. Admittedly, even if you land a paid position assisting a professor as an undergrad, the compensation is often not much more than minimum wage. While being a teaching assistant is not equivalent to industry experience and doesn't look as good on a resume, it can still serve as a stepping stone to landing your first internship, as any work experience is better than none. To land your first teaching assistant role, simply email the professor you are interested in working for. If they say no, email another and repeat as necessary. When emailing, ensure your message is well-written and concise, such as:

Dr. Last Name,

I am a sophomore majoring in aerospace engineering.

Upon review, I see you are teaching _____ this coming spring. I took that class last fall, earned an A, and was wondering if you were in need of a grader? If not, do you have any other opportunities available, such as grading for another class or overseeing a lab?

My resume and unofficial transcript are attached for your review. If you are interested in additional information or have any questions, please do not hesitate to ask.

Sincerely,
Justin Rittenhouse

In that example email, I stated my school year and major to give the professor a snippet of my background, which is highly relevant to the question I am about to ask. Next, since occasionally course offering lists can be incorrect, I am confirming the professor actually teaches the class I'm interested in being a teaching assistant for. This transitions nicely into asking if the professor is seeking a grader. Furthermore, I used that sentence as an opportunity to add additional information about my background. This time, the information is directly related to the job, as I stated I've taken the class and earned an A, thus providing the professor some insurance that I am qualified.

Perhaps the most important part of the example email comes next, where I ask about other opportunities. This can be crucial, as it can help the professor pause and think about other openings they may have available. Without it, they might have assumed you were only interested in grading that specific class or only interested in grading in general. However, providing this additional context opens the door for the professor to consider other opportunities they have to offer. Without this additional information, they may naturally just reply, "No, I already have a grader for _____. But I'll keep you in mind if the opportunity becomes available. Thank you." This indicates they gave little, if any, thought to your email. Often in life you'll find you have to help people think, especially when trying to achieve a goal for yourself. This isn't intended as a criticism of anyone; it's simply an observation that people tend to focus on their own long-term goals rather than on those of others. This, coupled with the fact professors can be extremely busy, means that if you don't give professors clues to help them pause and think of ways to benefit you, they likely won't. They'll just decline your offer and move on to the next email. Finally, the last paragraph simply provides the professor with the knowledge that my credentials are attached, and s/he can reach out to me if needed.

Another type of academic experience that can be, though not always, equivalent to industry experience is working on a research project. Many universities are classified as research institutions. This means that professors must perform research on top of teaching classes. In addition to their own research, they often oversee research projects of several students. The reason is research universities require professors to publish research consistently through conference and journal papers. As a result, professors at research universities are often seeking students to be a part of their research team. The first step to joining such a team is to find a professor whose interests align with yours. To achieve this, view the faculty profile pages of your professors. These pages can usually be accessed by navigating to the faculty directory on your school's department website. (Using WMU and aerospace engineering as an example, one could perform a web search for: "Western Michigan University Mechanical and Aerospace

Engineering faculty directory.") Once there, simply select a professor to view their profile page. Within a profile page, and depending on your college, you may find the following: their published papers, research interests, current projects, curriculum vitae, personal website, work history, etc. If your college does not have profile pages, a scholarly search can be used to find their published papers. (This can be achieved by navigating to scholar.google.com and searching professors by name.)

Once you found a professor, reach out and ask to join their research team. Again, use the power of free labor to your advantage. Over time, if you do well, the professor may offer you an assistantship down the road (meaning you could eventually earn a stipend and/or school-funded ("free") college tuition). But until you prove yourself, your greatest attributes are your ability to work for free and your willingness to do tedious tasks. Regarding the selection process, professors are typically more rigorous in choosing students for their research teams compared to selecting teaching assistants. If you have a history of past academic success, you may be selected based solely on your resume and a well-written email. For those lacking past academic success, there are other ways to set yourself apart and make the professor eager to add you to their team. Perhaps the best approach is enrolling in a class taught by that professor. Then, of course, excel in the class by earning an A and exceeding expectations on the class project. This means spending a substantial amount of time and effort on the project, and making sure your project is significantly better than your peers.

Not only have I seen others join research teams after performing well in a course, but I have my own experience. In my case, I didn't seek out the professor, nor did I enroll in her class with the intention of joining her research team. But after performing well in her course, she asked me if I was interested in joining one of her research projects. I ended up joining, and she never even asked about my GPA, resume, or any other past measurement of my ability. Admittedly, professors recruiting students is more commonplace in graduate school; however, it can and does happen in undergrad as well. In either case, I would not rely on the professor seeking you out for a few reasons. First, they might not know you're interested in joining a research team. Second, they don't know where your research interests lie. Third, they may not be actively pursuing another team member. That said, if you demonstrate an exceptional ability, a willingness to work hard, and clearly communicate to the professor your desire to join their team, they'll probably be open to adding you as a team member. And remember, when you do communicate with a professor, your email should be well-written and concise, such as:

Professor LAST NAME,

I am a junior majoring in aerospace engineering with a strong interest in _____. I have reviewed your papers on the topic, NAME OF PAPER #1 and NAME OF PAPER #2; thus, I was wondering if this is still one of your research interests? If so, I would like to discuss any undergraduate research opportunity or any other opportunity you may have available, such as grading homework.

My experience related to _____ includes NAME OF CLASS, NAME OF CLASS, and my attached research paper: NAME OF PAPER. These experiences only confirmed my interest in developing a strong background with regards to _____. The current area of _____ that captures my attention is learning more about the complexities of _____. But I would gladly welcome any opportunity to expand my knowledge in the field of _____. Lastly, I would like to highlight some of my skills that could be beneficial to your research team: _____, _____, and _____.

I have attached my resume and unofficial transcript for your review. If you are interested in additional information or have any questions, please do not hesitate to ask.

Best regards,
Justin Rittenhouse

That email example is slightly long, but this allowed me to add more detail to give you ideas for your own email. For even more ideas, conduct a quick web search, as that should fetch far more examples. That said, you should still be concise. Every sentence should matter and add new, useful information. The reason for the conciseness is that professors are busy individuals and can receive an abundance of emails, and they simply don't have time to read about your life story, nor do they want to. With professional communication, it's generally a best practice to respect the reader's time by not adding too much or irrelevant information.

A good way to respect people's time is by spending your own time writing the email. Yes, the email should be short, but it needs to be well-written and thoughtful throughout. This requires time and effort; it is not uncommon for some to spend an hour or more crafting an email. I frequently rewrite sentences in many different ways, often focusing on one sentence at a time and experimenting with different word combinations, until I'm satisfied with the way it all flows together. Tools such as a thesaurus or AI can help reduce the needed time to write a proper email, but the process still involves dedicated effort. Please note that not all emails require this much time, most should be quick. But important emails aimed at advancing your career should be thought-out, and this requires time.

Next, we will review the example email line-by-line with information explaining how every sentence adds value. After that are examples of sentences that don't add value to your email and should be avoided. Additionally, you should avoid including anything negative. For example, if your grades aren't great, don't attach your unofficial transcript. All professors are different, some may require a transcript and some may not. Thus, if grades aren't your strength (yet), wait for the professor to ask for a transcript before providing it. To be clear, never lie or hide anything, but you don't have to highlight areas in your performance that still need improvement. Highlight your strengths!

Breakdown of every sentence in the example email:

1. Professor LAST NAME,

   - It's just standard practice to include some type of greeting to the top of emails. You could also use "Dr. LAST NAME" as well. Just don't use Mr. or Mrs., regardless of whether your professor holds a PhD or not.

2. I am a junior majoring in aerospace engineering with a strong interest in _____.

   - This gives the professor three pieces of information: grade level, your major, and your interests.

- Also note, many students believe you have to wait until you're a junior or senior until a professor would have an interest in you joining their research team. This isn't true; you can get involved at any grade level.

3. I have reviewed your papers on the topic, NAME OF PAPER #1 and NAME OF PAPER #2; thus, I was wondering if this is still one of your research interests?

   - Research roles require in-depth literature reviews. By reviewing a couple of your professor's papers, it shows you understand the importance of a literature review and, at least to some degree, how to perform them. It also shows the professor you're willing to put in the work when no one has asked you to. Thus, you're not just trying to earn a paycheck; you're a hard worker and this is an area of genuine interest for you.

4. If so, I would like to discuss any undergraduate research opportunity or any other opportunity you may have available, such as grading homework.

   - This sentence is the whole reason for the email, and clearly stating what you're seeking is always a best practice. In this case, you're seeking to work for the professor. And as discussed before, it's also helpful to suggest other ways you can contribute. If you only inquire about research opportunities, the professor may assume you have no interest in grading homework. Or, while reading your email, it may not dawn on them that they have an opening for a grader. And by the time they remember, they may have completely forgotten about your email. Therefore, when it comes to your career path, never be afraid to provide others with ideas that could benefit you. Naturally, it should be a two-way street and the idea should benefit the other party as well. But people can be incredibly busy, and something that may only offer a slight benefit to them might not instinctively come to mind when they read your email, even if it provides a major opportunity for you. Thus, help them think of it!

5. My experience related to _____ includes NAME OF CLASS, NAME OF CLASS, and my attached research paper: NAME OF PAPER.

   - If you already have experience in the field of interest, it is important to highlight it to let the professor know you have some background knowledge. Also, showing past interest in the same topic illustrates that you do have a genuine interest. Therefore, you're not fabricating the interest in an effort to secure a research opportunity.

6. These experiences only confirmed my interest in developing a strong background with regards to _____.

   - This sentence is optional, but it tells the professor you understand developing skills in a certain field takes time and effort, and that you are committed to putting in that effort. Moreover, it tells them your desire to learn more isn't superficial, as you have previous experience and your enthusiasm hasn't faded.

7. The current area of _____ that captures my attention is learning more about the complexities of _____.

- This sentence is optional and should be avoided if your email is too long. Although, it is an opportunity to show you have more than just superficial knowledge on the subject and shows that you understand you have to hone in your interests. For example, if you are interested in the human body, maybe specify which part. Since the human body is highly complex, it's a pretty broad statement to say you are interested in the human body. However, it is a fine statement to make, particularly at this point in your academic career. But if you are more curious about a certain body part, say it, especially if the professor is researching that same area. If you can, don't be afraid to use professional lingo and really specify your area of interest. For example, instead of "learning more about the complexities of the knee" say "learning more about the complexities of the anterior cruciate ligament during axial loading." Additionally, don't be overly concerned that narrowing your scope too much might make the professor uninterested. Perhaps the professor is working on a research project related to the anterior cruciate ligament that isn't published or even announced publicly yet. Consequently, this email would really hit home. If not, they may be willing to start researching it, knowing they have a student that is interested. Worst case, the sentence adds nothing to the email.

8. But I would gladly welcome any opportunity to expand my knowledge in the field of _____.

   - This sentence is optional and should be avoided if your email is too long or you didn't include the last sentence.

But the reason for this sentence is similar to what we just discussed: just letting the professor know you are open to ANY opportunities they may have, even if the opportunities don't fall perfectly in-line with your more specified area of interest.

- See what I did there? I basically said the same thing numerous times. Look at the email and see how many times I said I was interested in _____. Did you catch the redundancy when reading the email? Saying you are interested in learning more about _____ is great, saying it twice to really drive home the point is fine. But three or more times is a bit much. It's nothing more than fluff at that point because it adds nothing to the email. Consequently, your email should be worded differently than my example to help you AVOID USELESS SENTENCES! You need to value the professor's time. My example email was structured this way for a few reasons: to include more sentences as examples, and to show you just how easy it is to be redundant when you're not paying attention. So, no one should just copy my example email. Your email needs to be personalized by you.

9. Lastly, I would like to highlight some of my skills that could be beneficial to your research team: _____, _____, and _____.

    - This sentence is optional, but it is good practice to inform people how you can benefit them, especially if you're seeking their assistance in a way that benefits you. Moreover, don't limit yourself to just field-specific skills here, such as CAD for engineering; also consider listing unique skills others may not have but could be beneficial for a research group. For example, if you're a machinist, or at least have the ability to make simple objects out of metal, list it in the email. It is not uncommon for a professor to need someone with the ability to design and build items, such as test fixtures. In academia, a machinist skill set can be more valuable than you might realize. This is, of course, true for other skills as well.

10. I have attached my resume and unofficial transcript for your review.

- Depending on the email client used by the professor, attachments can be hidden on the bottom of emails. Therefore, this sentence just lets the professor know you included attachments, and they should look for them.

- As discussed before, don't include information that doesn't highlight your strengths. If you are still working on improving your grades, don't include your unofficial transcript. Professors understand people can have strengths that are beneficial to society (and research teams) that don't necessarily correlate to a high GPA.

11. If you are interested in additional information or have any questions, please do not hesitate to ask.

- Admittedly, this sentence isn't really needed, as the professor knows they can email you back. However, in professional communication, it is standard practice to inform the reader that they are welcome to reply with any follow-up questions. I suppose this is an exception to the rule of "No useless sentences."

Sentences to avoid:

1. I think you're a great professor.

   - This information doesn't add anything to the email and is already assumed, given that you're asking to work for them.

2. My name is _____.

   - Your email address probably already displays your name. If not, it will be in your signature.

3. How much does it pay?

   - In industry, of course pay is important, and taking a job without knowing the pay would be foolish. However, as an undergraduate researcher your value is highly limited and you should be willing to work for free, at least initially. Therefore, either ask subtly about pay or let the professor bring it up, if there is any. If there is no pay or it wasn't discussed, then down the road, after you have established a good working relationship with the professor, you can consider revisiting or addressing compensation. Additionally, at this point, the professor would be far more willing to help you find an avenue for compensation if they lack available funding themselves, such as writing letters of recommendation for scholarships and/or grants.

4. I'm a transfer student from _____.

5. I was on the football team.

6. My high school was _____.

5. *Why gaining experience matters and how to do it*

- Sentences 4 through 6 should be avoided because you don't need to include unrelated background information. Again, these emails need to be concise, and you need to value people's time!

7. My parents donated $X amount of money to this school.

8. My parents are engineers.

- Sentences 7 and 8 should be avoided, as there probably isn't a valid reason to mention your parents in these emails. It's fantastic your parents donated money to the school, but that's irrelevant. It's also irrelevant what your parents do for a living. The professor would be adding *you* to their research team, not your parents.

9. I didn't do well in your class, but _____.

- Bad classes happen; there is no reason to highlight them. Plus, if you don't mention it, the professor probably won't even know, as they manage too many students to recall everyone's grade. Honestly, depending on the size of your college, they may not even remember you. Of course they could check to see what grade you earned in their class; the question is: Will they? And the answer to that is dependent on the professor. In summary, just avoid volunteering nonpositive information. Highlight your positives! Additionally, any excuse you have for your poor grade is likely one the professor has heard a thousand times before. Thus, they won't buy it, nor will you get any sympathy points, whether it's true or not.

5.3. Clubs, associations, and professional societies

Another fantastic way to gain experience is by joining clubs, associations, and professional societies, but their availability is university-dependent. At Western Michigan, there were a plethora of options which ranged from creating a Baja car and racing at national Baja SAE (Society of Automotive Engineers) competitions to a Raspberry Pi Club. Typically, real-world experience still outweighs the value of these societies; however, they can still provide a valuable stepping stone to landing your first internship, as these societies allow you to gain skills and experience using industry-standard tools and engage in real-world problem-solving. Thus, you'll be developing a skill set that future employers will covet. In addition, these societies often have room for advancement. This means that your hard work could lead to a leadership role, which obviously looks fantastic on a resume. One of the best parts of these societies is that they usually don't have grade level requirements, meaning you can join one your freshman year. If you do well, in a few years you could become the president of that society.

In addition to being a resume builder, there are several other perks to joining a society. One such perk is free travel, as these societies often have to travel for competitions, and depending on the society's available funding, your travel expenses (including food) may be covered. Another perk is the network of professional contacts you can create while participating in these societies. And as we will discuss next in Section 5.4, never underestimate the value of a good network, nor the amount of doors it can open. This network won't just include students from your school either, but will also include professors from your school, as well as professors and students from across the globe. This is because societies generally have one or two professors as supervisors, and competitions can be global.

One way to discover the societies or clubs available at your school is to just pay attention, as many societies post signs to attract new members. Another way is to do a quick web search to see if your school has an online list (search for "clubs at NAME OF UNIVER-SITY"). For those still in high school, ask around, as there may be similar options available. One example is the VEX Robotics competitions, as these competitions help you build soft skills like teamwork while also enhancing hard skills in mechanical engineering and computer science.

5.4. How to land your first internship

The easiest way to get an internship is through your network; this advice also holds true for your future career as well. Simply put, having connections can do more for your career than a good GPA, attending a good school, or almost anything else you do. Now, don't misunderstand me, those other items matter, but a connection is by far the quickest path to getting your foot in the door. In fact, you would miss out on most job opportunities if you don't use your network, as it's estimated that 70% of jobs are never published on publicly available job search sites.[33] In addition, up to 80% of all jobs are filled through networking.

I saw the power of networking at my first internship, Denso. Their policy was to fill internships and co-op positions with family members first. Consequently, many of my friends that were interns or co-ops at Denso either had family there or were a friend of a Denso employee. In short, you needed a connection to land one of their internship positions. Although I didn't have family or friends who worked there, I did manage to form a connection ... by selling a treadmill on Craigslist. The lady who bought the treadmill just so happened to be a recruiter at Denso. While it wasn't family or friends that got me my first internship, I still got it through networking.

The same is true for my co-op at Denso, which I obtained since one of the directors of the test lab knew me from my time as an intern. When he had an opening, he called me to see if I was interested and offered me the co-op position before anyone else. If I wanted it, all I had to do was say yes, and I did. Thus, I didn't have to compete against hundreds or even thousands of applicants, many of whom could have been more skilled or qualified than me. Thankfully, I had the best qualification of them all: I knew the guy. Additionally, he knew I was a hard worker and had a good personality. Anyway, I have heard Denso removed their family-first policy, which is good as it was clearly flawed. However, for better or worse, nepotism will always be a part of the workplace.

As my career expanded to different companies, I found that the relationship between networking and landing an internship position didn't fade. In fact, the first company I worked for as a full-time engineer only hired football players from Western Michigan University or children of current employees as interns. Why football players? The network that existed, of course, included the general manager of the company, who had ties to the football program. My next employer had one intern while I was there, and he just happened to be the cousin of the lead engineer. In summary, I have been in the working world for a while now, and although it's not impossible, at times it certainly feels impossible to find an intern or co-op who earned the position based solely on merit. I hope my stories help emphasize the importance of networking. If they do, then make sure you're asking yourself: Who do I know? Who do my parents know? And who do my extended friends and family know that could help me land an internship? You should be asking yourself these questions, even if your network lacks connections at your dream company. It's still valuable to have a fallback plan.

Another approach to landing an internship or co-op is obvious. However, I'll say it for the sake of completeness: apply. The time to start applying is in early September of the year prior (note: some companies may even begin accepting applications as early as the summer before). For example, if you are seeking a summer 2025 internship, you should begin submitting applications in September 2024. You may have noticed I said applications and not application. That is because applying for one, or even a small number of internships, may yield poor results. And if it does, don't feel bad, as everyone gets rejected. As a result, you should be applying for numerous internships, even internships you don't want. The experience at any internship is invaluable; it will help you land a better internship next summer. (Remember my experience with a Blue Origin recruiter from the beginning of this chapter?) The value of an internship is long-lasting, too. For example, tech firms seem to love internship experience, as evidenced by the high percentage of employees with past internship experience at companies like Google and IBM, at 78.3% and 70.1%, respectively.[34]

An additional method to land an internship or co-op offer is by participating in job fairs. These events are held regularly at most colleges, and provide a great way to meet with recruiters face-to-face, making them a great opportunity to shine. Though before you attend one, you need to prepare. First, update and then print off a dozen or more copies of your resume, as each recruiter you speak with will ask for one. (It's a good idea to use a padfolio/portfolio to store your resumes at job fairs, as it looks more professional than walking around with a stack of paper.) If you want to stand out more, consider alternatives to plain white paper. For instance, you can head to your local office supply store and have them print out copies of your resume on nice, thick paper. Obviously, paper quality won't land you the job by itself, but it will almost certainly be noticed and is a great conversation starter. Next, do your research and learn background information on the companies you're interested in. A fantastic starting point is to review their job listings and find openings for internship/co-op positions. Review them thoroughly, consider what they are looking for in an intern, what the job descriptions say, the qualifications they seek, the requirements they have, and the skills they desire. Once you have that information, write down how your skills and past experiences directly correlate to each of those questions. This way, when you're at the job fair and recruiters are asking you questions, your answers will directly relate to the position they're trying to fill. Remember that when recruiters speak with you, their goal is to gather information to determine if you're a good fit for their openings. Thus, help them out and make it blatantly obvious you're the best fit!

If you want to step your approach up a level, create custom versions of your resume for each company you're interested in. If that's too time-consuming, simply make unique resumes for the internships and co-ops you truly covet. Personally, I had two base resumes, an engineering resume and a programming resume. Then, depending on the type of job I was applying for – engineering or programming – and after thoroughly reviewing their job posting, I selected one of my base resumes and modified it to best fit the job description and qualifications based on my past experiences. This includes incorporating the same keywords found in the job postings into my resume. And just to be clear, when I say modify your resume, I'm not saying to lie, as you should NEVER lie. You can, however, correlate relevant information to match an opening. Alternatively, you can remove nonrelevant information that doesn't match the opening, as there's nothing wrong with tailoring your resume or having multiple versions of the "same" resume. In fact, if you are applying for high-end internships (or high-end jobs in general), you better tailor your resume to each position you apply for. In some cases, you almost need your resume to convey that your entire working and academic life has been focused on gathering the skills and experiences necessary to make you the perfect fit for that internship (or job). For example, if you're applying to a company that is seeking an intern to build CAD models, then CAD should be prominently featured repeatedly throughout your resume. Furthermore, include as much in-depth detail as is reasonable with regard to your CAD experiences and skills. (For instance, consider the following questions: What have you created, excluding any confidential information? Did you work as part of a team? How complex were the drawings, such as the number of components involved?) In addition to updating your resume to emphasize CAD, start considering how to answer questions, as your answers at the job fair (or during an interview) should emphasize your CAD experiences as well. Finally, as you prepare for the job fair, don't forget that you need to dress well. The rule of thumb is you can't overdress, but you can underdress. To find job fairs hosted by your school, a simple web search should suffice (e.g., search for "job [or career] fairs NAME OF UNIVERSITY").

Lastly, if you're unable to land an internship, which may prove difficult for freshmen and sophomores, you should consider spending the summer as a factory worker, as factories are typically always hiring. This is especially beneficial if you're an engineering major, as you'll be manufacturing the products you may someday be designing. Even if the products do not interest you, you'll still gain valuable manufacturing experience. This includes establishing an understanding of how products are actually manufactured, which is useful information across countless lines of work. This experience will also improve your chances of landing an internship next summer, especially with the company where you worked, as you now have valuable insight into the manufacturing side of their products and business. Not only is this considered a huge plus, working on the floor demonstrates that you're willing to put forth the effort required to succeed. Moreover, you often interact with engineers on the factory floor; thus, you'll be creating a network with actual engineers within that company, which will skyrocket your chances of landing an internship there next summer even more.

But by far, the biggest benefit of working on the factory floor – especially for those of you fortunate enough to have a more privileged life – is the ability to work hand in hand with factory workers and actually get to know them on a personal level. This will help you get below the surface-level relationship that often exists between blue-collar and white-collar workers. This disconnect can be quite significant; at times, it seems like office employees forget that factory workers are human, too. While this last benefit may not contribute much to your career, it may contribute a lot to your personal growth and make you a better person.

5.5. How to build a strong resume

Now that you know how to land an internship, it's time to learn how to create a strong base resume to maximize your odds in a competitive job market. Notice that I used the term "base" resume. This is because, as mentioned in Section 5.4, often your resume should be tailored to the position for which you are applying. The tips provided in this section have helped me land interviews with high-end companies and can hopefully do the same for you. In addition to these strategies, know that many universities offer programs or hold events focused on helping you strengthen your resume. I strongly encourage you to use these free programs. Given that college is expensive, you might as well take advantage of their resources, especially those that can potentially increase your income (through improved internships and career opportunities). And, of course, numerous online resources exist that can also aid you in crafting a strong resume. To assist in your resume-building efforts, I'll share my thoughts and advice for each item within the following list.

Key elements of a strong resume:

1. One page and boring

2. Education, work experience, and academic experience

3. Soft and hard skills

4. Certifications, achievements, awards, and professional memberships

5. Contact information

6. Check for spelling mistakes, grammatical errors, and readability

As an undergraduate, there is a high probability you don't have the experience to warrant a resume longer than one page. Even if you feel like you do, you probably don't, and I would strongly advise against it. What you need to understand is that, on average, recruiters take six seconds to review a resume.[35] This is because they have an endless amount of resumes to review, and plenty of candidates that are as equally qualified for the position. Therefore, if your resume is too long or too fancy, they won't be impressed, and they may just skip it. To avoid being "too fancy," include no photos, no splashes of color – your resume should be simple, boring, and in black and white.

With regards to writing your resume, remember that less is more – be concise, except when using acronyms or other lingo that might not be clear to a recruiter. Industry-standard acronyms are acceptable to use (e.g., CAD for computer-aided design), but most others should be spelled out and placed in parentheses following the text (e.g., Justin is Awesome (JIA)). This is because acronyms that seem obvious to you might not be obvious to others. Additionally, ensure to include only relevant information without being redundant. Relevant information includes work experience, education, and academic experiences, and does not include hobbies or interests. Work experience should include what you did, what skills you developed/improved, what company you worked for, the company's product, employment start and end dates (including both the month and year), job title, promotions, awards/recognitions, and how you improved the company. Optionally, you may want to include the industry (food, automotive, etc.). When stating the information, bullet points are recommended where applicable, even though they take up more room than a long paragraph. However, they look cleaner and are easier to read. Moreover, if you have had multiple jobs, list them in reverse chronological order.

Next is a snippet of my work experience taken from an earlier version of my actual resume. Notice how the bullet points break up the writing and enhance the readability when compared to a block of text (e.g., this paragraph). If your resume is formatted with dense blocks of text, it may get ignored, as eye breaks are generally desired.

- Oversaw all RFQs (Requests for Quotes) for customers on new and current products, including multi-million dollar contracts with Fortune 500 companies.

- Managed the engineering department; this included signing off on all engineering change notices (ECNs), working with our sales team, creating CAD drawings, assigning tasks to others.

- Assisted customers through the product design process (i.e., from brainstorming to creating prototypes to ordering).

- Evaluated all continuous improvement activities, implemented plans to optimize performance and processes (5S/Kaizen/Lean).

- Implemented our new EDI/ERP system (EDI/HQ and Job-BOSS).

- Developed Python scripts to automate tedious office tasks and convert JobBOSS output files into user friendly files. Implemented open-source programs to assist with day-to-day needs of the company.

- Created new machines and modernized old ones from spare parts, and assisted in repairing broken machines.

- Assisted across all day-to-day functions of running the company, including Accounting, AP, AR, Customer Relations, Production (OEE reports), Purchasing, Quality (PPAPs, PFMEAs, Control Plans), and Shipping.

Note that this snippet of my resume isn't perfect, far from it. A few shortcomings include the need for improved acronym usage, a failure to state the company's product, and (if the job I'm applying for uses SolidWorks) the omission of SolidWorks within "creating CAD drawings." Additionally, some of my bullet points are too long. Even on the resume itself, some of these bullet points spanned over multiple lines. Long bullet points can be acceptable, but single line bullet points are preferred. Moreover, the bullet points cover too many aspects of that role. It's fine to include all these bullet points in a base resume; however, when I was using this resume to apply for jobs, I should have removed bullet points that were not applicable to the job I was applying to. But my biggest failure was a lack of quantifying and impactful information. It needs to be clear to recruiters and hiring managers that you make an impact. Examples of impactful bullet points that I have since added to my resume include "Engineering achieved a 100% on-time RFQ rate" and "Led the design of an innovative manufacturing line, increasing throughput up to 50%." In summary, learn from my mistakes.

One aspect that is often overlooked, but is important, is the order in which you arrange your resume. I prefer to list skills and education first, as they are relevant and short. This allows recruiters to quickly verify that your desired bachelor's degree aligns with the position before moving on to review your experiences. Next comes either industry or academic experience, determining which one to list next depends on which aligns best with the requirements of the position. If you have previous internship or co-op experience that directly relates to your field, then place industry experience after education. However, if all of your prior jobs are unrelated, such as stocking groceries, then place academic experience, such as relevant school projects, after education. This is because grocery stocking experience provides limited relevance to the company compared to your academic experience. In fact, once you acquire enough field-specific industry experience, you'll eventually remove all nonrelevant jobs from your resume to respect recruiters' time. While nonrelevant jobs provide useful insights – such as demonstrating a willingness to work, longevity, promotions, and soft skills – this information will eventually become apparent through your relevant work experience as well.

Additionally, make sure to organize your bullet points. Those most relevant to the position you are applying for should be at the top. For example, if I were applying for a programming role, of the bullet points listed earlier, the bullet point starting with "Developed Python scripts ..." would be my top bullet point for that position. Moreover, I would elaborate even more on that aspect of the job. I would even delete many, if not all, of the nonrelevant bullet points to make room. Basically, bullet points should be arranged in decreasing order of relevance, while maintaining a logical flow. (In some cases, a less relevant bullet point may need to be placed above another to maintain coherence.)

Soft skills can be challenging to include in a resume and are often overlooked. But these can generally be embedded throughout your work and academic history. For example, if you want to highlight your leadership ability, you may want to include a bullet point that starts with: "Led a team of five fellow freshmen to..." As far as deciding which soft skills to embed, review the job posting and try to align your resume with their requirements; using the same or similar wording and phrasing can be beneficial. As a example, if they list "Must have the ability to work in a fast-paced environment," then you may want to include a bullet point that states: "Managed all quotes in a fast-paced environment (automotive), while maintaining a 100% on-time quoting rate."

With regard to hard skills, undergraduates commonly list them alongside their perceived skill level with terms such as proficient, great, good, etc. Honestly, I did this too as an undergrad, and it's fine, as many students still classify hard skills in this manner on their resume. Therefore, this is more of a preference item, but I no longer use that classification system, as those terms mean very little since one person's "prolific" could be a more experienced person's "bad." Furthermore, your skill level will either improve or decline over time, depending on whether or not you continue to actively use that skill. Thus, you may end up having the word "prolific" next to a CAD program you haven't touched in years. An alternative approach is to create two lists: "Currently working with" and "Past experience with." This approach may not necessarily be better, but it does simplify grouping of skills. It also indicates to the recruiter that skills under "Currently working with," you could start using on day one and be productive, while skills under "Past experience with," may require a little bit of time before you would be productive. And if a recruiter wants a self-assessment of your skill levels, they can always ask during the interview process. But often a self-assessment is not necessary since you should be including any skills listed in the job posting that you possess in your respective industrial and/or academic experience sections of your resume. This tells the recruiter how you actually acquired and used the skills, which is far more useful than your biased opinion of yourself.

When I did use the self-assessment approach, I genuinely believed I was being honest. I truly thought I was proficient, and I'm sure you do, too. Nevertheless, over time, you'll realize that there is plenty of room for growth with regard to any of your skills. Recruiters understand this, and they know that skills are developed through consistent use over a long period of time. This is why recruiters ask questions like: "What did you use _____ on?," "How many past experiences do you have using _____?," and "Describe your most in depth experience using _____. Also, what was the original goal, and what was the outcome?" Those types of questions tell a recruiter a lot more about your skill level than your opinion. This line of questioning also reiterates the importance of having hard skills within your experiences, as it tells recruiters the answers to these questions before the interview, or at least gives them a rough idea.

With all that said, I don't believe the skills section adds significant value to a resume. Again, companies care about proven productivity. Therefore, under the skills section on my resume, I simply list relevant skills in one line, separated by commas (e.g., "CAD (AutoCAD and SolidWorks), CAE tools, R&D, Project Launch, Project Management, Teamwork, Manufacturing, Problem Solving"), as I assume the recruiter skips over it quickly. The main reason I even keep the skills section on my resume is to help get past applicant tracking systems (ATS), as the skills section provides an easy way to include keywords from the job posting. To populate my skills section, I review the job posting and try to determine what skills matter most for the role. Then, based on what skills I have, I fill in my skills section from what I perceive to be the most important to the least important until I hit my one line limit, as I prefer to not have my skills section span multiple lines.

Certifications, achievements, awards, and professional memberships should all be on your resume as well, if relevant. These are a great way to stand out from the crowd, show you consistently try to self-improve, and constantly push yourself to learn more. All of which are traits coveted by employers, as they don't want employees who merely go through the motions. Additionally, you should include memberships to clubs and associations on your resume, as they showcase the traits previously mentioned, demonstrate your ability to apply academic knowledge to real-world situations, and highlight your willingness to work as part of a team.

Your resume should also include the following contact information: your name, an email, and a phone number. Some recommend including your address as well, but I feel addresses are too personal to share with the world. Thus, I only include my city and state. Lastly, ensure to quadruple check for spelling mistakes and grammatical errors, as these types of errors can be people's pet peeves. But even for recruiters who understand you're human and mistakes happen, it still creates a negative impression that could have been avoided. When checking for mistakes, pay attention to the readability of your resume as well. This means ensuring that items are in the correct order and that the writing flows smoothly.

With regard to cover letters, I don't have much advice as I don't think they're particularly useful. The advice I do have is simple. If it's a job you highly covet, then write a cover letter. For all others, don't waste your time. This is because writing them should never hurt your chances of landing an interview; however, in most cases, it won't help either. In fact, a survey of 10,000 recruiters found that 61% said cover letters do not matter, while another 8% were indifferent.[36] I believe the vast majority of cover letters are never read, and a compelling resume is your ticket to landing an interview.

5.6. How to ace your interview

Now that you have the knowledge to craft an outstanding resume, it's time to build on that by learning how to ace the interview process. With this expertise, you'll be well-equipped to earn that coveted internship. Next is a list of the steps you should implement before the interview, followed by a breakdown of each item.

Preparing for the interview

1. Research the company

2. Study the job description

3. Prepare a list of questions

4. Create a list of projects

5. Practice your answers

6. Dress for success

7. Bring copies of your resume, a padfolio, and pens

During the interview

1. Listen and take notes

2. Practice good manners and body language

3. Be authentic, positive, and confident (not arrogant)

4. Tie your answers to your skills and accomplishments

5. Focus on how you can benefit the company

6. Ask questions

7. Maintain composure (and avoid appearing desperate)

Always research the company before your interview. A couple of great starting points include their "About Us" page on their website or their Wikipedia page. An hour or two of research should be enough at this level, as interviewers would never expect you to know endless amounts of information about their company. Honestly, background knowledge of the company rarely gets brought up in interviews. In fact, I've only been asked to share what I know about the company a handful of times, and each time, they were only looking for a brief overview. More often than not, it's me squeezing knowledge I know about their company into the conversation, as an attempt to demonstrate that I did my due diligence. Anyhow, there are still other valid reasons to research the company beforehand. First, it's good to confirm the company aligns with your morals. Normally this isn't an issue, but if you have strong moral beliefs, it could be. Second, as just discussed, it allows you to incorporate information about the company into your responses during the interview. Lastly, it helps with crafting interview questions that tie in your skills and experiences with their work. (For example, "I saw a(n) COMPANY's NAME video on how they designed _____; it appeared the designers used NAME OF CAD SOFTWARE. NAME OF CAD SOFTWARE was not listed as a requirement for this role. However, with my past experience, it caught my eye. Is NAME OF CAD SOFTWARE a program I could be using as an intern?")

After reviewing the company, you should review the job description and take notes on how your skills and accomplishments directly correlate to their requirements and qualifications. Personally, I print off the job posting and make a note next to each requirement and qualification. For those that I meet, I state how I meet them. For those I don't, I state the skills and experiences I possess that I believe best relate to that specific requirement or qualification. If you don't have anything that remotely aligns with a requirement, then take the time to research that requirement. That way if it comes up in the interview and you're interested in it, you could say something along the lines: "While I don't have prior experience with _____, I have researched _____, and believe that it is a skill I would love to develop." Thankfully, with this approach, it shouldn't take more than 10 to 15 minutes to research the requirement since you're going to admit you don't have experience. Thus, interviewers will not expect you to have a strong understanding of that requirement, nor will they ask in-depth questions about it.

Alternatively, an even better approach exists, especially if you're enthusiastic about the role and the requirement appears to be highly important for it, and that is to gain experience. Of course, this approach is only feasible if you have the available time. But if you do, there are a ton of free tutorials available across the internet for basically everything a STEM student might need to learn. (YouTube is a great resource.) To grasp the basics of a skill, just work your way through a couple of tutorials. To gain a more in-depth understanding, think of a project that excites you, then do it. Accomplishing a project with no step-by-step tutorial will develop that skill to a much greater level of proficiency than merely replicating someone else's work. You will struggle, but through those struggles you'll truly learn! Then, at the interview, you can explain how you developed that skill by successfully completing the project. Note that the project doesn't have to be anything too elaborate, either. It can be, if you want and time allows, but it can also be as simple as a project you can complete in just a few days. With regards to the difficulty, a limiting factor to keep in mind is the amount of time you have available before the interview. Of course, if the project interests you and you wish to pursue it further after the interview, then by all means pick a very challenging project. Fortunately, since it's not a school project, you'll probably be able to avoid writing a report, which should save you a considerable amount of time.

Moreover, don't forget that any new software program you may need could be freely available through your college. If it does not appear to be available within your school's computer lab, just ask the staff managing the lab; they may be able to provide you with free access. This is because colleges grant access to certain programs based on students' majors; however, they are normally willing to add programs to your account if you request them, and they have them available. An additional reason to ask is that colleges often install certain programs only in specific locations or on specific computers. Thus, the staff managing the computer lab should be able to look up that information.

Ultimately though, if you don't have a "required" skill, nor the time to develop it, it's important to keep perspective and not panic, as often "required" skills are not actually required. If at this point you're wondering why they're called "required," for that I do not know. Often though, if you have a majority of the listed "required" skills, you're typically in good shape, especially at the internship level. Of course, the more the merrier when it comes to having "required" skills. However, your personality and past examples of exceptional ability will go a lot farther than a few missing "required" skills.

After, and during, your background research, it's important to prepare a list of questions to bring with you. When creating the list, remember to leave space between each question for notes and answers during the interview. One of the biggest benefits of creating this list beforehand is it eliminates the difficulty of generating thoughtful questions on the spot. Moreover, don't feel obligated to ask every question on your list. This is especially true for the questions that the interviewers have already addressed during the course of the interview, as that may make it appear that you were not paying attention.

Regarding the questions, you should have a good mix of general, job-specific, and company-specific questions. Additionally, it's a good idea to have questions about and for the interviewers themselves. Don't be afraid to look up their LinkedIn profiles and form some questions about their careers and career paths. (E.g., "I saw on LinkedIn you worked at company X for several years. What influenced you to apply here?") With regard to preparing all question types, don't forget to use obvious resources like the internet to help you find and develop great questions to ask. This includes the company's website and the job posting. If you are generally interested in the role, this should naturally inspire thoughtful question ideas out of pure curiosity. Reviewing the job posting also helps ensure that your questions are not already answered within it, as asking a question with an answer clearly stated in the job posting may reflect as poor preparation. One important question to ask at the end of the interview, if it hasn't already been addressed, is about the next steps in the hiring process and their expected timeline for hiring. This question is important because it shows you are excited and interested in working there, and it can also help ease your anxiety. For the latter, this is because their hiring timeline could span weeks or possibly months, even after your interview. And, as the saying goes, "waiting is the hardest part." Thus, knowing when to expect a response can alleviate some of that anxiety. It also provides you with a timeline for when to follow up with the recruiter after the interview if you haven't heard back. Alternatively, if it is well past their stated timeline, and given that it's not uncommon for companies to fail to inform candidates, you can assume you were not hired and you can move forward with other opportunities. To help assist with questions, a small sample is listed next to use as nothing more than a starting point.

List of example questions to ask during an interview

1. What can I expect during a normal day, week, or month?

2. How do you evaluate interns, and what will I need to accomplish to be considered a great intern?

3. On average, what percentage of interns are offered full-time careers at Jia's Engineering upon graduation?

4. How would you describe your management style?

5. Why did you choose to work for Jia's Engineering?

6. Can I see the current state of the project I would be working on?

7. How would you describe the culture here?

8. What do you value most in an intern?

9. Are there any concerns over my potential fit for this role?

10. What are the next steps in your interview process? And what is the average timeline for this process?

Next, make sure you have a detailed list of your past and active projects. By detailed, I mean to include information you think an interviewer may ask, such as what was the goal, what was the final outcome, how did you approach the project, what tools did you use, what challenges did you encounter, how did you overcome them, etc. This list will prove to be invaluable during the interview, as it is common for interviewers to ask in-depth questions about projects, especially if they relate to the job. For example, if one aspect of the job involves helping to design a complex piece of equipment consisting of hundreds of components, the interviewer may ask, "Give an example of a time you designed a complex system of parts? And, during the process, what challenges did you face, and how did you overcome them?" This is where a premade list can be beneficial, as it helps you avoid having to recall projects on the spot and, inevitably, forgetting to recall a highly relevant project. Additionally, you can review the list before the interview as a helpful refresher. This enables you to sound more knowledgeable and confident about the projects during the interview. Ultimately, the main goal of this list is to eliminate overthinking, unnecessary awkward pauses, and forgetting about relevant experience. Lastly, don't be afraid to provide copies of your list to the interviewers, as there is simply no better way to showcase your capabilities than through past work experience.

Before the interview, you should practice your answers to common interview questions as well. (These types of questions can be found all over the internet.) While most interviewers may ask only a few, if any, of these types of questions, it's still beneficial to be prepared to save on your response time. This helps to eliminate creating an excessive amount of awkward pauses, as you will certainly be asked questions you can't prepare for, and these types of questions will require thought. To be clear, taking time to gather your thoughts to provide an insightful answer is perfectly fine. Perhaps it's even recommended as it demonstrates your ability to think before you speak, but doing so for every question will make others in the room feel awkward. Thus, if you practice common questions and create a list of projects, you should be able to confidently answer most questions efficiently.

When it comes to researching questions to practice, don't spend too much time crafting thoughtful answers to opinion-based questions. It's useful to have answers for them, but focus more time and effort on preparing responses to questions that highlight your past experiences. As we have discussed, employers use past success as an indicator for future success. Reflecting on my own experience, I don't believe I have ever been asked, "What are your weaknesses?" or "What are your strengths?" The only opinion-based question I recall encountering, at least regularly, is, "On a scale of 1–10, how good are you at _____?" But, as discussed earlier, even that question isn't too common as your biased opinion of yourself is not the best indicator of your actual skill level. However, one reason this question is asked is that it helps to assess your relative skill levels. (That is, are you better at X or Y?) With that said, I'm not saying don't be biased, either. If you're trying to earn the job, and you believe you're an eight at a particular skill, say eight. If you can't decide between seven or eight, say eight. Don't lie or exaggerate, but there is nothing wrong with rounding up. When answering, the thing to remember is your numbers should be based off on your skill level relative to your classmates and not seasoned professionals. For those of you with industry experience, this might feel misleading. However, recruiters understand that a college sophomore rating their skill level as an eight is far less skilled than a professional with 15+ years of experience rating themselves a seven. Simply put, they're two completely different scales.

Perhaps the most common interview question is, "Tell me a little about yourself?" Since this question is asked frequently, it's worth the time and energy crafting a good answer. We'll discuss this question in more depth shortly. Ultimately, when practicing answers to interview questions, always keep in mind the primary goal for any interview: to determine if the interviewee has a good personality and identify how their previous experiences, industry or academic, relate to the role. Thus, ensure your answers are geared with those in mind.

Moving on to clothing, the old saying applies here, and you need to dress for success. This entails wearing professional attire, as business casual is not good enough for interviews. For guys, this means a suit (pants and jacket), a button-down shirt, a tie, and nice shoes. Women, on the other hand, have more options with regards to acceptable attire; however, it still needs to be a professional outfit. Since I'm not a woman, I will refrain from offering my two cents on what is acceptable for women.

For my first internship interview, I had no clue what to wear, so I simply asked the recruiter, "What should I wear?" Her response: "You can never overdress for an interview." If you're worried about not being able to afford a nice suit, don't be. There are plenty of low-cost options for dressing well, such as purchasing a suit from a thrift store, buying secondhand clothes from friends or family, or borrowing from them. I bought my first suit jacket from a family member for only $20. It wasn't the prettiest, as it was brown with stripes, but I paired it with dress pants I owned, and secured my first engineering job wearing that thing. Later, once I had a little more money, I bought a cheap suit on Black Friday for around $100. At the time of this writing, nearly 10 years later, this is the suit I still use. This $100 suit was even good enough to land me a job with a Fortune 500 company, so please don't justify overspending on a suit just because you think you "need" it for job interviews. If you want and can afford to buy an expensive suit, then of course go for it. But you don't have to and as long as you look presentable, no one hiring for STEM will care about the name on the inside (the brand). Furthermore, it doesn't even have to be comfortable, as few STEM majors wear suits to work. Typically, business casual is the required dress code. This means you'll likely only wear it a few times a year, if that, and probably only for a few hours at a time.

On top of dressing well, and to top off your professional look, make sure to bring a padfolio. Within the padfolio, you should have a legal pad, a couple of pens, copies of your resume, interview questions, a list of projects, and answers to common interview questions. The legal pad and pens are for note-taking, and the justification for pens over pencils is that pens look more professional and their tips don't break. With regard to the resumes, at a minimum you need enough for everyone that you are interviewing with plus one for yourself. However, bringing a few additional copies is always a wise idea. While interviewers typically print off their own copies, I have been in interviews where interviewers forgot to print off a copy, and sometimes you have more interviewers than you were expecting. Thus, it's better to be prepared.

Moving on to your list of interview questions, this should be easily accessible so you can use it as you see fit. My preference is to bring it out at the end when the interviewers ask if I have any remaining questions, but some prefer to ask questions from their list throughout the conversation. (Note: This is just with regards to the list of questions, as everyone should be asking questions throughout the interview.) As for your list of projects and answers to common interview questions, these can be hidden within your padfolio. The reason you bring them is to do one last review right before the interview. For this, I usually arrive at least 10 minutes early. (Yes, I do the review in my car.) Additionally, you may have downtime during the interview process, which provides an opportunity to review them once more. Of course, your list of projects can also be used during the interview. And, as discussed before, having copies to distribute can be beneficial as well.

During the interview, ensure you're listening and taking notes. However, avoid excessive note-taking, as this isn't a class. Writing the whole time could be distracting to the interviewer and wouldn't come off well. Only write down key pieces of information, and typically use abbreviations while limiting the use of complete sentences. The goal is to capture just enough information to recall key discussion points later; you can always add more details after the interview. (Though, avoid waiting too long as the human memory can fade quickly.) There are many compelling reasons to take notes, such as using your notes to help create future questions. These questions can occur later in the same interview, during subsequent interviews within the same company, or in interviews with external companies. Building on that, if you have additional interviews within the same company, your notes will be a valuable resource for preparing. Additionally, notes can simplify the comparison between companies and can assist you in identifying which one is a better fit for you and your career goals. Lastly, taking notes demonstrates to the interviewer that you are invested and interested in the job opportunity.

Good manners and body language can also make a significant difference during the interview. Examples of good manners include saying "please" and "thank you," asking for an item instead of overreaching, not interrupting others when they're talking, cell phones being hidden and set to silent, holding doors open for others, being polite to everyone, and introducing yourself before sitting down. When it comes to having good body language, examples include sitting up straight, making eye contact, smiling, and having uncrossed arms. If you're questioning whether body language actually plays a role in your chances of receiving a job offer, consider this survey of senior managers who were asked to rank nonverbal cues based on how much these cues tell about a candidate. The rating system was from one (not much) to five (a lot). The survey revealed body language does matter and eye contact, posture, and handshake ranked as the top three most telling with scores of 4.41, 4.26, and 4.26, respectively.[37]

Remember to be authentic and true to yourself throughout the interview. If you try too hard to impress people or pretend to be someone you're not, people will notice in a nonpositive way and feel that something seems off about you. Therefore, be you! It got you this far so don't change now. This also means, don't be a robot, be human. It's perfectly acceptable to admit that you're nervous during the interview. Along with authenticity, your focus should be on the positives. This includes when speaking about previous employers, even if you strongly disliked the working environment or past co-workers. Fortunately, you can prepare for this, as questions regarding your previous employers shouldn't come as a surprise; after all, discussing past experiences is often the focal point of any interview. In line with that, one of the most common questions you'll be asked when interviewing for your second internship is, "Why don't you want to go back to _____?" This is the interviewer's way of either determining if similar working conditions exist at their company, which could cause you to leave, or probing just to see how you'll respond. So, again, you need to be positive, even if your experience was negative. If you can't possibly think of one positive – which I would be skeptical of – then focus on the experience you've gained (or skills you've developed) and the new opportunity. For example, say something along the lines of, "While I'm grateful to _____ for the experience, I believe NEW COMPANY is a better fit for my long-term career goals because ..."

Along with being positive, you need to be confident and enthusiastic without crossing the line over to being arrogant. Because once you cross that line, it's difficult to recover, and you probably won't get the job offer. In fact, 76% of recruiters will reject an applicant who comes off arrogant.[38] Thankfully, you can be both confident and enthusiastic without crossing the line, and you should be, especially when talking about your projects and the job opportunity. To do this effectively for the projects, talk in-depth about how much you learned and the skills you developed. Furthermore, don't say things like, "The project wasn't very good," "The project was kind of lame," or "The project wasn't really impressive." However, discussing ideas for future improvements is both acceptable and recommended. In fact, common interview questions are, "Knowing what you know now, would you approach the project differently? How would you improve the final product?" If faced with these questions, don't be foolish and say "nothing," as there is always something to improve. If you genuinely believe your project is perfect and couldn't be improved, then think about your electronics (computers, phones, etc.). They are created by billion- and trillion-dollar companies that employ highly skilled STEM majors, yet every year they come out with a new and better model (and have constant updates to add features and fix bugs). If they can't seem to make a perfect product, what are the chances you did? To be clear, this isn't meant to be a criticism of anyone. I'm simply stating, more or less, how the design process works: you create, you learn, you recreate – making it better – and the cycle continues.

Of course, when interviewing, you'll be tasked with answering a large variety of questions. When addressing these questions, tie your answers back to your skills, knowledge, and accomplishments as often as you can. This concept was briefly introduced earlier in the discussion about practicing your answers; now, we will go into more detail. To start, one question an interviewer may ask is, "Do you have CAD experience?" Don't just say "Yes," say something equivalent to: "Yes, I have used CAD in college to create _____ for class _____. In addition, at company _____, I was able to gain industry-level CAD experience. Through this experience, I learned significantly more about the use of CAD in an industrial environment, including GD&T, the importance of using standard-size materials to reduce the machinist's workload, the advantages of standardizing parts to reduce inventory and costs, and the concept that just because you can design something in CAD doesn't mean you can make it in real life, at least without incurring extreme and unnecessary costs." By giving examples of your accomplishments and knowledge, you are making a clear statement about your ability. Without examples, the interviewer is left wondering about your true skill level and is relying solely on your word that your CAD skills are an 8 out of 10. And since the interviewer doesn't know you, why would they trust your word over someone who provides examples of past successes and expertise? Simple answer: they wouldn't.

Additionally, to enhance your response further, also tie it back to the job description and/or requirements. For example, if the requirements list SolidWorks and your experience is in SolidWorks, then replace the word CAD with SolidWorks in the previous example. Again, don't leave the interviewer guessing, make it as clear as possible that your knowledge and skills make you the best candidate for this opportunity. This includes when addressing this dreaded interview question: "Tell me a little about yourself?" The interviewer is not looking for an in depth breakdown of your personal life. While you may say a little about your interests and hobbies, limit it to only a couple of sentences. Then immediately return to providing the information they are actually seeking, such as your qualifications, why you applied for the role, and will you mesh well within their company's culture. Thus, talk about your past academic and work experiences, along with skills gained outside of those settings. Emphasize the skills you developed and improved that relate to the position, and highlight key responsibilities and achievements. Even nontechnical jobs may be worth mentioning, as they can demonstrate your soft skills. For example, I used to work at a grocery store. I could say something along the lines of, "My working career started at a grocery store. My responsibilities included cutting, filling, and stocking all produce while answering the phones and helping customers. This experience undoubtedly helped me improve my soft skills, such as working in a fast-paced environment and customer service." To give another example, if you're interviewing for a computer programming role, mention that you code in your free time for fun and bring up any personal projects you've completed or are currently working on, especially those that relate to the role.

Another important concept to remember when addressing interview questions is to focus on how you can benefit the company. While this is often achieved through the methods already discussed, it's just important to remember that the interviewer is not overly concerned with how this role benefits you. It's true they want you to be enthusiastic, as excitement for the role will drive you to be engaged and work hard. However, there is no need to yammer on about how this is a dream role. At the end of the day, the interviewer has the company's interest (and their job) at heart, not how amazing of an opportunity this is for you.

Since the topic of asking questions was discussed in detail earlier, we will avoid going into too much detail here. However, I'll say this again to reinforce the point: never forget to ask questions. This is because questions demonstrate to the interviewer that you're interested and engaged. Furthermore, they help create a positive dialogue. In summary, just ensure you're asking questions regularly; this should not be difficult if you're genuinely interested in the role (and if you came to the interview prepared).

Next, remember that during the interview it's important to maintain composure. I understand you may be desperate, especially if this is your first internship interview, and that's fine but don't show it. It simply never comes off well. This means to avoid rambling and nervous chatter, remaining calm and concise, and ensuring your interviewer has time to speak. This also means to ensure you consciously limit your jokes if you're a nervous joke teller. It's acceptable to sprinkle in the occasional joke, as this is a good way to settle your nerves and encourage a friendly dialogue. However, telling too many jokes will come off as unprofessional and convey that you're not taking the interview seriously. With that said, it's still important to read the room before telling any jokes, as some interviewers won't find any humor appropriate. (Lame, I know.) It's also important to keep all humor PG and never to joke about your willingness to do anything for the job. Even if the latter is true, never say it since it reeks of desperation. It also implies you may be seeking any job offer and are not interested in a long-term commitment. This is a major red flag as employers seek employees that actually want the job long-term. This includes interns, as the ultimate goal of hiring interns is to find those worth offering a full-time position to upon graduation. If you are taking the interview because no one else will offer you one, that's fine but never admit it. It should appear that you are interested, and that the role is a good fit for your long-term career goals. While the interview may not be with your dream company, the reality is you should be excited about most opportunities, as any internship is better than none and can serve as a valuable steppingstone.

At this point, you may be wondering whether accepting a role at a company you're not interested in long term is unethical. I would strongly argue no, as it's merely a business decision, nothing more, nothing less. It's actually equivalent to the business decision the interviewer is making on behalf of the company. In that, they are trying to determine how hiring you benefits the company now and in the future. Moreover, if you want a "better" internship next summer, it's a decision that has to be made (recall my Blue Origin story from earlier).

If the interview is with your dream company, it's still important to avoid appearing desperate. It's fine and recommended to appear passionate about the opportunity, but don't cross the line over to brown-nosing, as it comes off awkward and not genuine. This means never say something similar to: "_____ is my dream company, and I have always wanted to work here. I love everything you do. I can't believe how lucky I am to receive an interview." While saying one or two of those sentences may be fine, overall that statement is excessive. A better approach would be to say something similar to this: "I appreciate your time and am thankful for this interview since _____ is known for being an excellent company. Additionally, this role aligns well with my career goals of becoming a(n) _____." Notice the "known for being": This is because you haven't worked there, and you don't know their inner workings. There is nothing wrong with acknowledging their good reputation, but it tends to be best to avoid making absolute statements, especially if you haven't verified them yourself.

When it comes time to schedule the interview, remember that companies want employees that stick to their commitments, especially those that involve other people. Thus, don't be selfish by dropping all prior obligations, as delaying the interview will not impact their hiring decision (assuming they did not explicitly state they are on a tight timeline to conduct the interview). To be clear, I'm not saying to delay the interview just to appear busy, nor am I saying you shouldn't drop unimportant tasks or rearrange your schedule to accommodate the interview. I'm simply stating it's fine to acknowledge your busy schedule and, in most cases, delaying the interview a week or so will not be an issue. This delay also allows extra time to prepare for the interview itself.

Moreover, don't be overzealous with thank-you emails after an interview. In fact, I wasn't even going to recommend writing them, as I've had better luck receiving job offers without them. However, that could be merely coincidental, as research does back the use of writing thank yous. For example, 68% of recruiters and hiring managers say follow-up emails impact their decision-making process. Furthermore, of those surveyed, 16% admitted they have completely eliminated a candidate because they didn't write a thank you after the interview.[39] Thus, armed with that knowledge and the fact it's unlikely to harm your chances of receiving a job offer, it is probably a best practice to write thank-you emails. With that said, keep in mind that the rules of not looking desperate and valuing the recipient's time still apply. This is because recruiters and interviewers can receive an overwhelming amount of emails, especially during the hiring season for internships and co-ops. So, keep your email short and to the point to increase the chances of it actually being read rather than skipped or, at best, skimmed. When writing, try to consider it from the recruiter's perspective: imagine if all potential interns wrote long emails. There simply wouldn't be enough time in the day to read them all, especially when you consider recruiters have other responsibilities.

While it's never too late, try to send thank-you emails within a couple of days. As far as writing the email, an example of a real thank-you email I sent can be seen after this paragraph. Additional free examples can be found online through a web search. But remember, these examples should be used as nothing more than references to get you started, as your thank-you email needs to be genuine and written independently. Honestly, it isn't that hard. Just remember when actually writing the thank-you email to highlight your skills that would benefit the company, to tie your points back to the interview to demonstrate your attentiveness, to reaffirm your interest in the role, and to encourage the interviewers to reach out if they have any additional questions. Of course, the last item is nothing more than a formality, as interviewers are well aware they can reach back out if needed.

_____ and _____,

Thank you again for creating time to meet with me Friday. I appreciated the opportunity to learn more about _____ and the current Systems Software Engineer opening.

Based on our conversation Friday, I feel I would be a fantastic match for a career at _____ due to my history of developing unique skills to become a more well-rounded engineer (e.g., Python, Linux, the ability to read and understand documentation, etc.). But more importantly, my mindset for continuous improvements. This

kaizen mindset appears to be the normal culture around
_____.

Lastly, I want to reiterate my interest in the position.
After Friday, I was more enthusiastic about the opportunity because both of you verified the company supports
my interests in becoming a more well-rounded engineer
and the ability to constantly learn/improve.

If you have any questions, please do not hesitate to ask.

Best Regards,
Justin Rittenhouse
Email: _____
Phone: _____

If I were to critique myself, the email is a little long. Thus, a
sentence or two should be removed and/or condensed. A good place
to start would be the sentence beginning with "Lastly, I want to
reiterate...," as the next sentence relays the same information: I
want the job. Regarding the next sentence, I should have said "I
am" instead of "I was." And for some reason, I felt a strong urge
to remind them the interview was Friday. However, I should have
avoided the redundancy. On a closing note, remember there is no
perfect thank-you email. Just do the best you can, and remember,
authenticity shines through best!

In closing, when (not if) you get rejected, don't feel bad. It happens to us all, a lot. The truth is that it's a competitive world and
sometimes the competition wins. The reasons could be they knew
the hiring manager, were an internal candidate, or were simply a bet-

ter fit. Unfortunately, what you will probably do is play a guessing game in your head and replay the interview, believing if you would have said this differently or that differently, you would have landed the offer. This is almost never the case. While there is always room for improvement, the fact is magic words do not exist. Often in life people search for magic words; they believe if they find the right set of words, things will go their way. That is not how the real world works. People are complex and have their own thoughts and opinions, meaning no matter how well you craft a response to a question, it will not resonate with everyone. Some may love your answer, some may like your answer, while others may dislike your answer. This means, regardless of what some influencer says, there is no exact statement you must make nor any question you have to ask. Simply do your due diligence and come to the interview prepared; if you do that and you still do not land the job, take some solace in knowing it wasn't because you worded a single answer wrong or didn't ask the specific question the interviewer wanted you to ask. Just remember, even failed interviews are valuable learning opportunities that help you improve your interviewing skills.

Chapter Bullet Points

- Real-world experiences are tremendously beneficial

- Help people help you, give them ideas that benefit you

- Tailor your resume to the job posting

- Demonstrate to interviewers how strong of a candidate you are by providing relevant examples of past success

- Magic words do not exist

Notes

6. Develop your soft skills

Soft skills are often undervalued by undergraduates due to the common misconception that if they excel in their field, everything will work out for them. This simply is not true. While talent and credentials may help you land the interview, it's often your soft skills and personality that play a significant role in your career trajectory, as they ultimately land you the job and promotions. Here's a fantastic quote from Elon Musk on how he used to overvalue talent in the hiring process:

> "One of the worst hiring mistakes that I've made in the past is looking too much at their intellectual capability alone and not on how they affect those around them. ... And it really matters if they have a good heart and personality" – Elon Musk

Undergraduates also commonly believe that the interview process is an evaluation of talent. That is only true to some degree, as interviewers are also tasked with determining if you are a cultural fit. This is because most people spend a significant amount of time with their co-workers, and companies try to foster and maintain high morale. This, in return, helps keep productivity high and leads to a reduction in employee turnover. As a result, regardless of skill, not being a cultural fit often means you won't receive a job offer. In fact, 92% of employers admit soft skills play a vital role in determining if an applicant should be hired.[40] Even if you are hired, you may not keep the job for long without soft skills. This is because 48% of new hires fail within 18 months, and of those failures, 89% (!) are due to a lack of soft skills (and only 11% due to a lack of hard skills).[41] The truth is, having a good personality isn't even difficult. Here are some key elements to remember:

1. Be kind and always keep your cool

2. Be humble and recognize your knowledge is limited

3. Never take undeserved credit

4. Listen, be interested, and be supportive

5. Have a positive outlook and a good sense of humor

Being kind and keeping your cool should be obvious, as no one wants to deal with rude/temperamental people. Thus, don't be one yourself; life's too short for that. Moreover, fewer people will want to help you or see you succeed if you're rude.

Next, it's important to remember to stay humble and to recognize the limits of your knowledge. As you progress through undergrad, you may reach a point where you start to believe you know a lot about your field. The reality is there is still so much you don't know. There's an old quote which speaks to this: "PhDs know a lot about a little." Basically, there is an infinite amount of information out there for every specialized branch within a STEM field. To demonstrate, let's use mechanical engineering as an example, which can be divided into subsets that include, but are not limited to, aerodynamics, controls, and structures. Each one of these subsets can be further divided according to industry. For example, an engineer may claim to specialize in structures, but do they work on aircraft, automobiles, medical devices, spacecraft, watercraft, or in another sector? This can still be divided further, especially if the engineer works for a large company. Let's assume the engineer works on aircraft; what part of the aircraft does he work on – wings, landing gear, etc.? All that to say, an engineer can spend their entire career designing aircraft structures and achieve world-class expertise. However, despite some overlap, they would struggle to design structures for medical devices when compared against even a novice engineer in that field. (At least, they would struggle without help and/or extensive research.)

This concept of understanding that there is always infinitely more to learn is another compelling argument for pursuing higher education. This is because one goal of education is to place you on the other side of the Dunning–Kruger effect, helping you recognize that learning is a continuous, lifelong process. Once you're there, you also tend to be a lot more humble. Furthermore, with enough life experience, you'll come to realize you have been wrong a lot, even on topics you felt confident about. This is fine, as being wrong happens to the best of us. Sometimes you're even wrong just because the information itself has changed, as humans are constantly making new discoveries and innovating.

This concept of recognizing the limits of your knowledge is why one aspect of continuous learning is understanding the importance of seeking and receiving feedback. This is because the person providing feedback may possess insight or information you lack, particularly if they have more experience. Unwillingness to accept feedback – also called "being defensive" – is actually why 30% of new hires fail.[41]

This one should also be obvious, but never take credit for someone else's work. If anything, do the opposite and share credit when, perhaps, you really didn't need to. In the long haul, people won't remember many details of a project, but they will remember if you took credit for work you did not do. In a group project, it is always better to say terms like "we" or "us" instead of "I". In addition, you should always listen, be interested, and show support towards all ideas. This isn't just for group projects but for life in general. People want to be heard and supported. If you have a better idea, that's fantastic. Though, make sure to listen to other people's ideas and avoid interrupting them. There should be an "every idea is a good idea vibe" within your group. Of course, every idea is not actually a good idea. Some ideas are bad and that's ok. But remember that some ideas that seem incredibly bad on the surface are actually fantastic. If the only cost is a little bit of time, you should even look into and test some of the "bad" ideas. I don't know how many times I said "Well, I certainly didn't think that was going to work." Some of those so-called "bad" ideas either turn out to be game changers – or, at the very least, they can often lead to great ideas.

Lastly, always try to have a positive outlook and try to see the humorous side to life. A little comic relief can really improve camaraderie and make a group project more enjoyable. Also, remember that nonverbal signals are important, too. Don't be that person who sits in the group with their arms crossed and shoulders slouched. This is because having a positive outlook and appearance not only improves your happiness but can also motivate other group members to work longer and harder, ultimately leading to better grades and results. (But always remember, even a failed project is a learning experience.)

In addition to a great personality, it's important to have a good foundation of other soft skills, such as the ones listed next. These are a great way to ensure good grades and to advance your career. Remember, we live in a society; therefore, no matter how great you are in your field, you have to be able to work in a team and be able to present your results and accomplishments well.

1. Communication and teamwork

2. Presentation skills

3. Adaptability

4. Creative thinking

5. Time management

Communication is the driving force behind every great project and relationship. Often, people will assume everyone is on the same page, even when they are not. The same way you don't know what other people are thinking, people have no clue what you're thinking. Great minds do NOT think alike; they think very differently. Thus, great communication encourages a good working environment, ensures transparency, facilitates coordination, and increases efficiency. All of these are key aspects to a successful project. I have seen it more than once where two people in a group unknowingly work on the same part, or a group member does something completely different than what the rest of the group was expecting. These kinds of mistakes can and should be avoided with clear communication and ensuring everyone has a clear objective of what they are expected to have completed between now and the next group meeting. (Group meetings should be scheduled regularly.)

If someone doesn't have their part complete at the next meeting, do not get angry. Instead, find out why. It's human nature to make assumptions with a lack of real evidence, but there are a myriad of valid reasons someone could not complete a task on time. One possibility, which you might not have considered, is that their role was more complex than it initially seemed. Therefore, it is always important to find out why they missed the deadline. With that said, if missing deadlines becomes a trend for a group member and it becomes clear they aren't even trying, then it is time to take action.

At this point, you may go to your professor and let them know. They may help, or they may let you know in the real world you will have to deal with uncooperative team members. As a result, the professor may force you to deal with it internally. Perhaps, a better approach is asking the team member what specific skill set they have, and what part of the project they would like to work on. If you can better utilize their skill set and make the work easier and more enjoyable for them, they may be willing to do more work. This may involve you performing a task you have no experience in and may not enjoy, but just think of it as a learning opportunity. I understand that it feels unfair that another student will have an easier job and will likely spend less time on the project than you. And you know what, you're right, it's not fair. However, that's life. Worse yet is the fact you will probably receive the same grade. Despite all of this, always stay positive and remember that even if you both received the same grade on one project in one class, this one grade means little relative to your or their long-term career goals. Take solace in knowing your future is brighter.

After completing a group project, you'll often have to present the results. To help you succeed, here's a list of tips addressing some of the most common mistakes made by undergraduates when it comes to presentations.

1. Avoid extra words

   a) With presentation slides, less is often more in terms of the number of words on a slide. You do not want your audience reading the whole time. They need to be listening to you.

    i. Slides are meant to emphasize your point and your speech. Don't make slides match your speech; that's redundant.

b) Don't use paragraphs; instead use bullet points, graphs, pictures, and videos.

    i. Remember, "A picture is worth 1,000 words," and it is significantly easier to show your audience something than trying to explain it.

2. Do not read from the slides

a) Your attention should be on your audience. Think about all the great speeches you have seen. Did they turn their head back every ten seconds to read from the slides? Probably not. Practice your speech and have it memorized. Not having to think on the spot improves your confidence and helps remove awkward pauses. A good tip is to use the bullet points on the slides as talking points, meaning anything important should have a concise bullet point to remind you to talk about it.

b) Notes are fine to read from, especially on long speeches. However, most classroom presentations are 10–15 minutes. I found that for these speeches, notes aren't typically necessary. This is especially true if you follow what I just said: Practice and use concise bullet points. For me, when I switch between slides, I read the new slide for a fraction of a second to jog my memory on talking points. If you have good, concise bullet points, no one will ever know you looked back (or down) at the new slide during the transition between slides.

3. Graphs over tables

   a) Graphs make it easier for your audience to visualize data and see trends quickly.

   b) Make sure your labels include units.

   c) Graphs should be easily read from the back of the room. (This is true for all content, as the audience in the back of the room need to be able to see your slides without issue.)

   d) Make sure your graphs are clear and avoid compacting too much information in one slide.

   e) Avoid manipulating data, even by accident. For example, be careful when using different scales when comparing graphs or having a zoomed in graph. If you do change the scaling when comparing graphs, ensure that your audience is aware of the change and understands the reason behind it.

4. Be energetic

   a) The best way to connect with your audience is having your passion shine through.

   b) I know nervousness can make this one hard. But try to remember you are not alone; 77% of people have some level of anxiety with public speaking.[42] Some people hide it well, and won't admit it, but most are nervous and have anxiety. The first class I taught had around 70 students, and trust me I was nervous. Heck, so nervous my armpits were sweating. Thankfully, I got through it alive, just like you will during your next presentation. To this day, I still have a little anxiety speaking in front of a new audience, but I kind of enjoy it now. Public speaking is like anything else, the more you do it, the better you get. With enough repetition, your anxiety fades and the nerves die down.

5. Avoid going over the allotted time

   a) Time is allotted for a reason. Often, when presenting information in both the working world and academia, you are given a time slot. It is rude to cut into someone else's time.

   b) There is a good chance your audience knows your allotted time. I have been in and to many presentations, and typically the second the presentation starts to run over is the second you start to lose your audience.

   c) I have yet to see a single professor give extra credit for going over the allotted time; however, I have seen some threaten to take points off if you do.

Adaptability is a trait you must possess as a STEM major. In the real world, projects change over time, or you may be reassigned to new projects. This includes moving to projects where you may lack experience. Thus, you must learn to adapt quickly. The best way to develop the adaptability trait is to take on projects you don't know how to do. Oftentimes when professors let students select their own project, undergrads will pick something they know a lot about. While this is easy, it does not develop new skills. Students need to realize college projects provide a great opportunity to learn new skills, as they come with the added benefit of receiving credit and feedback from an expert. So, instead of developing new skills on their own time, students should develop skills on "school time." Note: If you want to tackle a project well outside of your comfort zone, fantastic; however, make sure to discuss the project with your professor first. This allows the professor to make sure the scope of your project is reasonable for the allotted time. In addition, if a good professor knows you are pushing yourself, and are outside of your comfort zone, they know the quality of your work may dip. Consequently, they will often adjust their grading scale to ensure you get the grade you deserve. To be frank, some professors may even grade easier on you because it's clear you are putting in extra effort. Of course, we have to acknowledge some professors won't care and won't grade differently, which further emphasizes the importance of speaking to them first.

Similarly, for group projects, group members often pick a task they have experience in. While this can be a good approach in industry, it isn't the best approach for college. As just mentioned, college should be about trying to develop a wide range of skills to help you discover what you enjoy most while also making yourself more marketable. As a result, a better approach for group projects is for everyone to select a task they know little about. This creates the ultimate learning environment. This allows you to develop a new skill(s) while having people to lean on for questions. In addition, these people are your group members; therefore, they have an invested interest in helping you succeed.

Moreover, succeeding in any STEM field requires you to be a creative thinker. The whole idea of being an engineering major is to think outside the box to improve on current designs or create something new altogether. Remember, there is ALWAYS a better way to do something. It may not be the most obvious way, but you must always be engaging in *kaizen*, the continuous work of improving whatever you are working on. Unfortunately, often an idea you believe is better is actually worse. Nevertheless, if you truly believe it to be better, you must explore the idea. If it doesn't work, you can always go back to the old way of doing it. Words you'll hear a lot as an engineer are: "We have been doing it this way for X years." You'll hear this all the time, and yeah, it still annoys me to this day. And yes, the same person who said that will be the very first person to say "I told you so" when your idea does not work. However, do not let their shortsightedness deter you. Just remember to remain positive and that if it were not for people like you, who are trying (and failing), we would all still be living in caves. Innovation requires failure. And don't worry WHEN you're wrong; you weren't the first and certainly won't be the last person to utter or attempt something "dumb" or incorrect. For instance, a notable example of incorrectness was when *The New York Times* published an article on October 9, 1903 stating it would take one million to ten million years to create a "flying machine."[43] Even better, the article stated: "No doubt the problem [of creating a flying machine] has attractions for those it interests, but to the ordinary man it would seem as if effort might be employed more profitably." Good thing the Wright brothers didn't listen to such nonsense, as they took flight in their "flying machine" just 69 days later. And as we know today, air travel is quite profitable.

> "There's a silly notion that failure's not an option at NASA. Failure is an option here [at SpaceX]. If things are not failing, you are not innovating enough." – Elon Musk

Creative thinking does require time and effort, and as a STEM major, you will be in a constant battle against time. Therefore, it's important to develop time management skills. Some of these skills are probably obvious, such as prioritizing important projects or projects with closer deadlines over others. But where I see people lose the battle against time is in smaller tasks within a project. For example, I have seen people spend half a day (or more) on making an Excel document look immaculate. If that document is to be handed in and graded by the professor (or for customers in the working world), fantastic, well done. If this document is for your boss/supervisor, that's probably a good thing, too (depending on your boss). If this Excel document is for peers only, why spend so much time on it? Are you trying to show off? Know your audience. Don't allocate precious hours to tasks that truly don't make a difference on the outcome of a project. Treat time as the valuable resource it is. To be clear, I am not suggesting you make a horrible document in the name of saving time. You're making a document for a reason, presumably to pass along information, so you need to spend enough time on the document to make it easy to read. If it's not easily readable, it would probably cost you and your peers even more time due to the questions they'll have. Or worse, your peers could misinterpret the information. Thus, make sure everything is clear and readable, but above that, any time spent making a peer-to-peer document look pristine is wasted. Of course, in industry, this may not apply depending on your boss's desires, but in school, just make peer-to-peer documents clear and readable. And, for goodness' sake, don't spend hours and hours making a document look amazing that is for your eyes only. If you want to do that, perhaps to better your skills in a particular program, do that when you're not in school and time is plentiful (e.g., summer or winter break).

Another common mistake is not using the time you do have. Often, students will do projects and homework the day before they are due. Admittedly, I was guilty of this. The first problem with this approach is that it leaves you no time to ask the professor or other students for help if you encounter a challenging problem. Without help, the task can end up taking significantly longer. Even if help isn't needed, people tend to underestimate how long tasks take. I developed a good rule of thumb for this: First, try to think of all the steps required to complete a task or project. Take your time, as there are often more steps than you initially think. Once you've identified all the required steps, estimate how long it will take to complete them. Then, double that time estimate. I found the doubling method works well for me. I tend to complete projects in one and a half to double the time I think it may take in my head. This is because, like many others, everything just seems so much easier in my head, or I don't think of everything up front. But additionally, life throws you curveballs, and you're going to have hiccups, often even on tasks that seem the easiest in your head. The doubling method may not work for everyone; thus, experiment with it. Maybe for you, you need to triple your time estimates because you're really optimistic. It's far from an exact science. With all that said, even if you use the time doubling method, still don't wait until the last minute to do the project/task if you're able to avoid it. It unnecessarily adds a layer of complexity WHEN something doesn't go as planned. Instead, still calculate the time you believe it will take you to complete the task. Then, try to complete the task in that amount of time as soon as your schedule allows. The reason it's still beneficial to calculate the time you think you need, even when you do the task ahead of time, is so you have a target time to hit. Aiming to complete a task within an allotted time frame can help you avoid Parkinson's Law, which states that work expands to fill the available time allowed. For this reason, I don't recommend multiplying the time you think it will take to complete a task by ten. You need to find a realistic multiplier that works for you and strikes a good balance. Plus, spending ten times longer on a project than you should will not make it ten times better, as diminishing returns will come into play.

Furthermore, ensure you are productive with the time you do allocate for a task. This means eliminating interruptions. For example, working by yourself with your phone off is a good start. If you do have friends who are equally focused, then it's fine to work with them, but keeping phones off or silenced can significantly improve productivity. This is supported by statistics too as the average office worker checks their social media accounts 77 times per day while at work.[44] I have seen it countless times, people on their phone for ten minutes, fifteen minutes, or even longer. Then, they work for five minutes and pick the phone back up. You're literally making the same task take over three times longer than it should. Just stop, focus, and get the task done. If you need to take a break from time to time, great. We all do. In fact, Florida State University found that productivity peaks when working in uninterrupted 90-minute intervals.[45] Therefore, if you want a break every 90-minutes or more, go for it. But every five to ten minutes is simply too much. If you are one of those people who can't stay off your phone, you have no one to blame but yourself for not having enough time to finish all of your homework.

Additionally, avoid working in an environment where you are less productive. I go to coffee shops, put in headphones to drown out the noise, and work. Heck, often I don't even listen to music and instead I listen to pink noise. Personally, leaving home allows me to be my most productive. It's my way of forcing self-discipline. This is because, at coffee shops, it's either work or sit there bored. At home, there are far too many distractions. Of course, it's nice to watch TV as you "work." But, unfortunately, I have yet to find a person who has mastered the art of watching TV and working. At least, when it comes to working on tasks that require thought. Often, you'll spend hours slowly working on a task that could have been completed in one tenth of the time had you focused and kept the TV off. Moral of the story: Experience with different methods for completing your work in a timely manner. For me, it's heading to coffee shops. Maybe that doesn't work for you, so find something that does. Self-discipline is tough, so find ways to make it easier.

6. Develop your soft skills

Chapter Bullet Points

- Your personality matters

- Understand there is always more to learn

- Try to develop many new skills during college

- Time is a valuable asset; treat it as such

Notes

_____

_____

_____

_____

_____

_____

_____

7. The importance of writing well

The ability to write well is a significant weakness for many STEM majors. I have graded and reviewed many papers at this point, and the good writers are often only good relative to other STEM majors. This is not completely our fault: as STEM majors, we get to avoid many of those pesky English classes. (That's probably why half of us chose STEM.) I, too, was a bad writer, so don't feel bad if your writing ability is subpar. I still don't claim to be great. However, I have improved significantly. I did not realize it was such a problem until grad school. Early on in grad school my advisor called me out, and asked me to make a conscious effort to improve my writing. Then he told me how his advisor gave him the same advice. Having the ability to write well is not a real issue until grad school because in grad school you are expected to write conference and journal papers and, obviously, you do not want to embarrass yourself. Additionally, all my grad school friends were also asked to improve their writing ability. So, if someday you're asked to improve your writing, don't feel bad as it's common.

Anyhow, to get ahead of the game, you should start making a conscious effort to improve your writing today! This includes those who don't plan on attending grad school. This is because plans do change, and someday your path may lead to grad school. But even if it doesn't, writing at a grad school level as an undergrad will impress your professors, thus almost guaranteeing A's on your papers and possibly opening doors for undergraduate research opportunities.

To enhance your writing, we will now discuss many useful tips. Note that some writing tips were covered in Chapter 3, but those tips were for writing a personal narrative. Here, we are discussing technical writing. (Some call it academic or scientific writing, but for the purposes of this book, we will use the term technical writing.) There is overlap between writing a personal narrative and writing technically, so I apologize in advance for any redundancy. Technical writing is the type of writing you should be implementing in your STEM classes, and it can differ from other types of writing. This means, if you are writing a magnificent book (such as this one), a poem, etc., some of these tips may not apply. (These tips are not in any specific order.)

1. Maintain objectivity

2. Avoid writing in first and second person

3. Read well written journal papers

4. Always write more than you need

5. Less is more, do not ramble

6. Eliminate unnecessary words

7. Quantify it

8. Do not misrepresent or manipulate data

9. Include raw data

10. Create an outline

11. Use transitional words and phrases

12. Use a thesaurus

13. Use a more appropriate vocabulary

14. Do not use contractions

15. Write the abstract last

16. Edit, edit, and edit

17. When able, receive feedback

Objectivity is an important aspect of technical writing. You want to avoid any biases and maintain a neutral writing stance based on facts and not opinions. To help maintain this stance, avoid writing in first and second person and just state things as they are (see Example #1). Though, if you do express an opinion, make sure it is clear that it is an opinion and still avoid using first and second person (see Example #2). In both examples, the first sentence is the one to avoid, and the second is the corrected sentence.

Example #1:

- I collected good data using a strain gauge.
- Data was collected using a strain gauge.

Example #2:

- The model had bad results because of _____.
- A hypothesis for the poor agreement between laboratory results and the computational model is _____.

For the first example, "I" and "good" both had to be removed. Using "I" is an example of writing in first person, while "good" was removed because it is not up to you to determine whether the data is good or bad; that judgment is left to the reader. Additionally, saying the data is "good" might suggest you were hoping for a specific outcome, which implies bias. For the second example, similar to the first, it's not your place to label the results as good or bad. Again, that judgment is left up to the reader, and stating the results are "bad" implies that you were hoping for a particular outcome, which could indicate bias. Instead, you could acknowledge that the results do not align well with expectations, such as those from hand calculations or laboratory data.

To help gain an understanding of what technical writing entails, read research journals that peak your interest. Not necessarily the format used in journal papers, as journals are designed to be concise without trivial information, but you should review the actual writing. Items to pay attention to include the logical flow of the writing, the use of technical terms, and the information the authors included. Learning correct terminology will not only give you terms to use when searching for other journal papers, but it will also help vastly improve your writing. For example, you may learn the term "computational expense," which sounds and reads better than "computer time." With regard to the information in journal papers, at minimum you'll need to include the same type of information (methodology, results, etc.). However, for undergrads, professors usually require a lot more detail than in a journal paper and different formatting (a cover page, table of contents, etc.). One reason for the extra detail is professors want to review the "trivial" information, as much of the "trivial" information for researchers is brand new to college students, thus leaving room for errors or misunderstandings.

To find journals to review, simply visit your college's library website or scholar.google.com. Note: When using sources outside of your college's library website, like scholar.google.com, you may find that some of the journals cost money. Though, if you use your college's internet connection to search for journals, many more will be available for free. Alternatively, you can simply look up papers you found on scholar.google.com on your college's library website. In addition, some journals on scholar.google.com will lead you to a login page. If you log in with your school email address, you may get the journal for free. Furthermore, if you cannot acquire free access to a journal paper using the previously stated methods, email your college library. They can normally get a copy for you, for free.

Overwriting and then removing information that doesn't add value to your paper can greatly increase the quality of your writing. Yes, I know it's tough to not use your hard work. I've been there, too. In fact, not only have I removed a good amount of content from this book, I have also removed a whole chapter. Trust me, it wasn't easy, but it was the correct decision. After all, the chapter was about explaining basic engineering concepts (forces, moments, etc.) in layman's terms. Is it useful information? Of course. Would it benefit some readers? Absolutely! But does it fit within the narrative of this book? Not really. As a result, the chapter had to go, regardless of how many hours I put into it. Unfortunately, students tend to leave nonrelevant information (obvious information, irrelevant background information, etc.) in their papers to make them longer, but longer does not mean better. Less can be more. This problem is often exacerbated because many professors enforce length requirements, which can lead to students adding fluff to meet those requirements. Fluff is generally bad since there is always more good content to be written, but that content takes deeper thought. One good strategy is to start your papers early; this allows ample time to reflect on what's been written and to develop new ideas to add. This means, when it's time for the final edit, you should be able to remove all the fluff and still have enough good content to meet any required minimum page count. Plus, as you edit, more good ideas will come to you, and, of course, you would add those in as well. We will discuss the editing process later in this chapter, but the goal is clear: Always write more than you need.

Another form of fluff to avoid is the use of excessive words, such as using ten words for something that can be written in five. Students do this regularly to add length to their papers. However, this is a bad idea. The saying goes, "make every word count." If the word adds no value, remove it from the sentence. Words such as "just" can often be removed without additional edits to the sentence. For example, "It just does not make sense." → "It does not make sense." Furthermore, wordy sentences can come across as poorly constructed. Thus, make a conscious effort to be concise. For instance, "I just bought my ticket to Dallas, and I will be there three days before Danielle's birthday." → "I will arrive in Dallas on July 26th." In that example, eight words were able to convey the same information as seventeen. If you're writing a novel, more words could help create a vivid picture for your readers. But in STEM, we are not writing novels or books; we are writing technical papers. Therefore, get to the point as soon as possible and avoid rambling. (Though, make sure to have enough detail to clearly convey your message, argument, setup, results, or key points.)

In technical writing, everything should be quantified. Relative words such as big, small, long, etc. don't convey enough information to the reader. How big? How small? Small to you may be giant to someone else (e.g., an engineer who works on nanotechnology). The sentence, "The yard was big," does not convey any useful information to a researcher. The sentence should read, "The yard was 100 sq ft."

or even "The yard was big at 100 sq ft." Now your fellow researcher knows the exact size of the "big" yard. I know most reading this would not call 100 sq ft big. But for people in New York, any yard is a bonus. Consequently, calling a 100 sq ft yard big would be justifiable to them. Therefore, remember that relative words have different meanings to different individuals and should be avoided or, at least, quantified in technical writing.

Moreover, when you do quantify your information, it is important to be mindful in how you present your data. For example, let's say Company A had 50 people leave out of 5,000, and Company B had 10 people leave out of 100 due to some unfortunate event. How misleading would a report be if a report stated, "Company A loses five times the number of employees compared to Company B due to fall out after an unfortunate event"? While technically true, it's clearly a misrepresentation of the data as it appears Company A faced a more severe exodus of employees, and the reader is left forming the wrong conclusion. It should be easy to understand how someone can misinterpret data when it is not presented in the right context and format. A better approach would be to say Company A had 1% of its staff leave while Company B had 10% of its staff leave. Using percentages here isn't perfect, but will suffice when discussing the issue within your paper. Although, it can still be portrayed as you attempting to mislead your readers since Company A is fifty times larger than Company B. Therefore, like in most cases, it's not exactly a direct comparison as there are underlying differences between companies of different sizes. These differences could have played a role in people leaving or maybe these differences didn't, and it was a fair comparison. Regardless, the point is since many people will have a radically different thought process than you, you will have no clue what a fellow researcher is thinking when they read your paper. Information you thought was insignificant, or didn't even think of, a fellow researcher may think is very significant. I learned a long time ago that trying to guess what other people are thinking, or will think, is a losing game. You're wrong far more often than not. Thus, it's important to include raw data from your research in your report whenever possible.

The method or location (e.g., the results section or appendix) of inclusion for the raw data is up to you, as there is no set way. You can use a table, such as Table 7.1, or you could use plain text, similar to the way I did a few sentences ago, in the story about Company A and Company B. (The sentence starting with "For example.") Or any other way you see fit. Depending on the scenario, the raw data can even be filtered to improve readability (see Figures 7.1 and 7.2). However, you must clearly state that the data was filtered, why the data was filtered, what filter was used, and how that filter was implemented. (For example, due to noise in the system caused by _____, a third order Butterworth filter with a cutoff frequency of 20 Hz was used on Figure 7.2.) At the end of the day, in most cases, raw data should be in the report; it should be clear and visible. However, to clarify, including raw data is not a substitute for forming your own conclusion. You still need to state your conclusion, and clearly state how you established that conclusion. (For instance, Company A appears to be more stable than Company B since only 1% of its staff left after an unfortunate event.) Nevertheless, you don't need to, nor should you, force other people to form your conclusion by hiding your raw data. Let them form their own conclusions, too. If – actually, *when* – someone has a different conclusion than you, just try to figure out why. Did you overlook something? Maybe they're factoring in, through their experiences, information you don't have. Or maybe, they just think drastically different from you (e.g., Republicans versus Democrats). Regardless, just use it as a learning opportunity. Finally, did you notice the way that conclusion example was written? It did not say, "Company A is more stable ..." but said "Company A *appears* to be more stable ..." It was worded that way because absolutes (always, never, etc.) should be avoided in technical writing. The world is a highly complex place, so even if you are relatively certain your statement is correct, in most cases, it's impossible to be 100% certain. So when writing, remember the old joke, "Never use absolutes."

Table 7.1.: An example of how to include raw data in table form

Companies	Total number of employees	Total number of employees that left
Company A	5,000	50
Company B	100	10

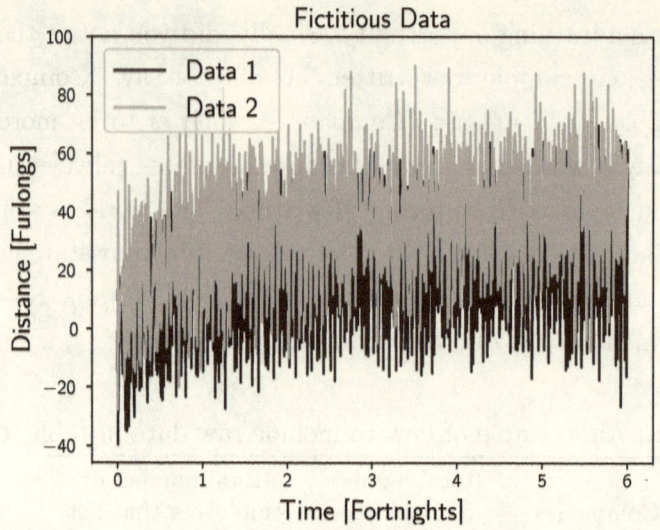

Figure 7.1.: Fictitious raw data

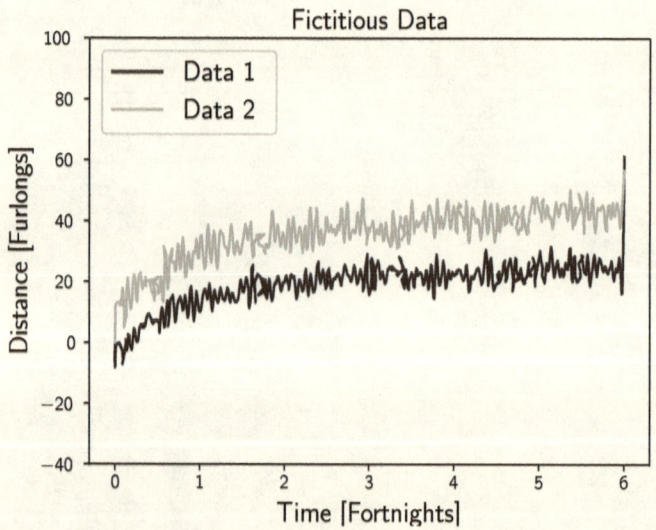

Figure 7.2.: Same data as Figure 7.1, but filtered via a 3rd order
Butterworth filter with a cut off frequency of 20 Hz

Because it is an important topic, let's discuss data manipulation a little bit more. Manipulating data is probably the best way to lose your audience and the respect of your peers. You truly need to stop and think every time you present data. Take a few seconds and ask yourself several questions: What is the best way to present this data (e.g., percentages, averages, raw numbers only, a table, a graph)? If you do choose to present the data in a graph, do the axes make sense? Are they to scale? Or have you stretched (manipulated) the axes to help prove your point? That could very well be data manipulation. You can see an example of this type of manipulation via Figure 7.3 and Figure 7.4. If you're wondering if this type of data manipulation actually happens in the real world, the answer is yes. In fact, Figure 7.3 is meant to mimic a real plot used as a marketing tool to increase the sale of Chevy trucks.[46] As you can see from Figure 7.4, where the y-axis is scaled correctly (0%–100%), their lead is far less impressive. Thus, yes, data manipulation is done heavily by mainstream media, marketers, salesmen, etc. But as a STEM major, you need to be better than that and hold yourself to a higher standard. The end goal is to have the data be presented in a clear manner that is easy to understand and, ideally, very hard to misinterpret.

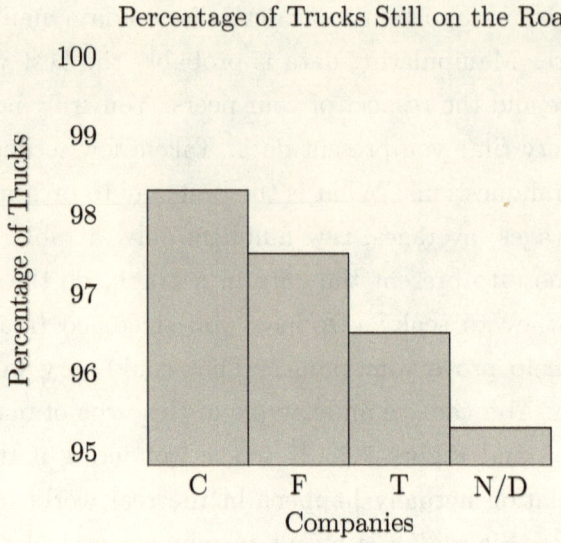

Figure 7.3.: An example of data manipulation

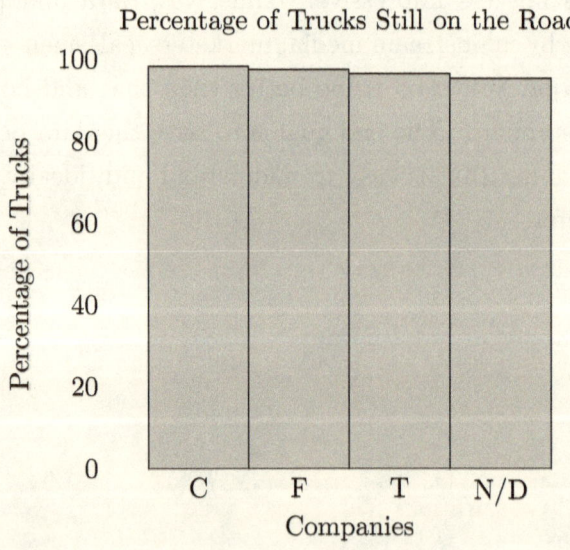

Figure 7.4.: Same data as Figure 7.3, but with the y-axis corrected

Moving on from data manipulation, let's discuss outlines as it can be wise to create one when starting a paper. If the professor gives you an outline, edit it and add far more detail. This is because a good outline helps organize your thoughts and ideas. This promotes smoother transitions between paragraphs and a better overall natural flow to the paper. Plus, it's always good practice to get ideas in writing as soon as possible. This is a lesson I have learned the hard way far too many times. I don't even want to know how many good ideas I've lost due to not immediately writing them down. Nowadays, if I think of a good idea, including ideas for a paper I'm literally in the middle of writing, I'll stop (for a second) whatever I'm doing, including writing, and write down a bullet point about that idea, so I can remember to get back to it later. If I'm out and about and come up with a good idea, I'll either email myself the idea or write it down via the notes app on my phone. As far as creating an outline, one method is to list out all the required sections of the paper. Then, within each section, create a topic sentence for every paragraph you plan on writing. Some believe this approach is best and can greatly improve the quality of your final paper. However, that's debatable, and this approach can be very time-consuming and may not be realistic for long papers. Thankfully, that isn't the only approach, nor is it the approach I use. I typically use one of the next two approaches. The first is to write down each section (introduction, methodology, etc.) with a gap between them to leave room for bullet points. Then I write down bullet points for everything worth discussing within the appropriate section's gap. The second approach involves creating a table of contents, and then writing down all the items worth discussing on a separate piece of paper. Often, I'll just end up doing a mixture of those two approaches. This is because I will have information I want to include, but I'm not 100% sure what section it should go in. Once you have the outline "complete," stop, reflect, and brainstorm new ideas. Ask yourself questions like, "What am I missing?", "Do I really need to talk about _____?", "What could make this paper truly standout?", etc. And don't worry if the outline isn't perfect, it's not set in stone nor is it going to be graded. Thus, you are free to move, add, or remove content as you write the actual paper.

Using transitions is a fantastic way to improve your writing. On the surface, transitional words and phrases may appear as a form of fluff and as the opposite of the advice from earlier, "eliminate unnecessary words." However, they are necessary since they help eliminate blockingness and provide a more natural flow to your writing by linking sentences and paragraphs together. For comparison, next are examples of sentences without, and then with, different types of transitions. What sentences do you believe flow better?

Example #1: To add information

a) My wife is lovely. She is nice and kind.

b) My wife is lovely. *Additionally,* she is nice and kind.

Example #2: To show cause and effect

a) I was late to work. My boss was mad.

b) I was late to work. *As a result,* my boss was mad.

Example #3: To contrast

a) The man worked hard. His business did not succeed.

b) The man worked hard. *However,* his business did not succeed.

Example #4: To emphasize

a) I have no problem with community colleges. I started out at one myself.

b) I have no problem with community colleges. *In fact,* I started out at one myself.

Example #5: To provide an example

a) Earning a STEM degree can increase your chances of succeeding financially. Engineers routinely make well over six figures.

b) Earning a STEM degree can increase your chances of succeeding financially. *For example,* engineers routinely make well over six figures.

I believe most would agree that the examples with the transitions flow more naturally. Besides the examples provided, transitions have a variety of other use cases, such as comparing, concluding, repeating, sequencing, changing topics, etc. Options to assist in finding transitional words and phrases to use in your writing include a thesaurus, a simple web search, and AI. (See section 11.3 for more detail on using AI.) Of course, moderation is key as too many transitions can cause your writing to lose flow and clarity.

Thesauruses should be your best friend as they can drastically improve your writing. Thankfully, there are free thesaurus websites online (such as thesaurus.com) or you can simply google, "SOME WORD synonym." Moreover, don't think that your vocabulary is so extensive that you don't need one. No matter how large your vocabulary is, it's still nothing more than a small fraction of the total number of English words used in circulation today. In fact, as of 2019, the Oxford English Dictionary contains full entries for 171,476 words in use.[47] However, most adults only have a vocabulary of 20,000–35,000 words (native English speakers). Let's pretend you can double the high end, and your vocabulary is 70,000 words; that's still less than 41% of the total English words in circulation.

Two scenarios where thesauruses really shine are their ability to dramatically reduce redundancy within your writing and help improve the quality of your word selection. For example, next you'll see two example paragraphs. Read them and ask yourself, Which one is better? Which one sounds more intelligent?

1. Very is a valid word. Thus, it can be used. Though, it is never good practice to use the same word very often. Thus, use a very good thesaurus.

2. Very is a *legitimate* word. Thus, it can be used. Though, it is never good practice to use the same word *repeatedly. Consequently, utilize* an *exceptional* thesaurus.

Even though the two paragraphs are almost identical in meaning, and only a few words changed, the quality of the second paragraph is undeniably higher. That's the power of a thesaurus. Additionally, did you notice how the first paragraph used the same word (thus) to start two sentences within a close proximity to each other. Read it again. Once you notice it, doesn't it have an awkwardness to reading it? That's why it's frowned upon. Therefore, use a thesaurus and avoid starting every other sentence with the same word. (Note: These two paragraphs also demonstrate how using too many transitions can add an awkwardness to your writing.)

When writing technically, not only should you use superior words, but it's also important to use an appropriate vocabulary. You should use words related to your field. Next are two examples illustrating the difference between using a typical vocabulary and using a technical vocabulary. I think it's evident that the second sentence in each example demonstrates the writer's expertise in their field far better than the first.

Example #1:

- The material was stiffer than planned.

- The material had a Young's modulus that exceeded expectations.

Example #2:

- The computer took too long to run.

- The computational expense surpassed the allowable wall time.

In addition, contractions, which are often two words joined together to form one via an apostrophe, should be avoided in technical writing. That is, don't use "don't", you can't use "can't", and it isn't ok to use "isn't." Instead use "do not", "cannot", and "is not." This is because contractions are viewed by many as informal and unprofessional; whether that's true or not is clearly opinion-based. However, it is the current consensus to avoid them, and assuming you want the highest grade you can get on your paper, I would follow suit.

Moving on to abstracts, note that it is typically best to write them last. I have regularly seen students try to write a paper from start to finish. This is generally bad practice; not only can you bounce around the paper when writing, you should, and abstracts are a prime example. Writing the abstract first generally takes significantly more time. Plus, once the paper is written, you'll probably have to heavily edit the abstract anyways. This is because abstracts are supposed to summarize the entire paper, and it's difficult to summarize a paper that hasn't been written. Therefore, complete the paper, then head back and write the abstract. This will save you precious time and energy. And remember, a good abstract includes your research problem/objectives, your methods, your important results, and your conclusion.

Edit, edit, and edit your paper some more. Editing and proofreading should be done numerous times. The easiest way for your audience to lose focus is a typo. Think about it: What happens when you notice a typo? You either reread that line or word two to three times to understand what it was supposed to convey, laugh at the error, or, in the worst case, end up with incorrect information. (For example, you might have meant to include "not" in a sentence, when it should have been included.) Ideally, you want to avoid all of these to the best of your ability. One method I use for editing involves writing a paragraph, proofreading that paragraph, then running that paragraph through a text-to-speech program. Note that these readers can be found for free online. (Of course, we should acknowledge that many of these free online programs are free because they take and use your data.) Then, significantly later, I read the whole paper again and use a text-to-speech program as needed. And, of course, I make constant little edits if I write more during the waiting period.

The reason I delay the final edit is to avoid the material being fresh in my mind. When the material is fresh, I know exactly what I was thinking, so my brain will often fill in missing words and make grammar corrections. Thus, everything makes sense and seems logical. However, once the material is no longer fresh, there may be parts of the paper that don't make sense. And if it's not completely clear to me, the author, those parts will make zero sense to someone else. But the best benefit of editing later is, as discussed earlier, the additional time to think of good material. I frequently think of good ideas at random, such as when I'm driving, taking a shower, or in the middle of the night. As a result, the longer I have between the first draft and the last draft, the more time I have to think, and the more high-quality content I can add. A great example of that is this book, as it took years to write. There probably hasn't been a single month where an idea hasn't popped into my head, actually, probably not even a single week. If I tried to rush this book, and knocked it out in six months, it would have been half as long, missing a plethora of good information, and filled with a lot more low-quality content.

As for the last point, as I edit I often remove material that I thought was good, but upon re-reading, I realize it was not. When you're writing and deciding what material to remove, keep asking yourself, "Does this add value to my paper?" If not, remove it. Furthermore, don't be afraid to remove some good content to meet (or go below) a page count maximum; there is nothing wrong with only having great content! (Also, don't ever feel obligated to hit a page count maximum. Again, less can be more!) Lastly, remember that once you earn that A, it will all be worth it, no matter how gut-wrenching it was to remove some of your hard work.

The reason I use a text-to-speech reader is that they allow "someone," in this case a computer, to read my paper to me. When reading my paper to myself, my brain will often fill in typos and grammatical mistakes. If I wait between edits, as previously mentioned, it helps me catch many of my errors; however, my brain still fills in a few. Whereas a text-to-speech reader cannot fill in these errors and will read them out loud. As a result, I find text-to-speech readers to be a better option than reading my paper out loud. (These programs are even more beneficial if you're writing a paper in your non-native language.)

7. The importance of writing well

Another way to drastically improve your paper's quality is having a more skilled writer proofread your paper. They will catch mistakes you won't, as some of the mistakes they catch you won't even know are mistakes. Consequently, not only does this method improve your current paper, it provides a great opportunity to learn from your mistakes and makes you a more skilled writer for future papers. If you need help finding a skilled writer, note that many colleges have programs where people will review and correct papers for free. Take advantage of these programs. Typically, your school's library will have information on these programs. Although, it is important to note these writers probably know little about the subject of your paper. They only help eliminate typos and grammatical mistakes. They cannot and will not tell you if you used the wrong equation or if you have any other technical errors. This is because your major is not their major, and in all probability, they won't have an in-depth background in your field of study. Moreover, there are free grammar checkers online. I have never used them to check a whole report, so I don't know how well they work in that regard. But I have used them to check sentences and paragraphs, and they seem useful but not perfect. Another way to help eliminate errors is to copy your text into Microsoft Word or Google Docs, if you're not already using them, as these programs have built-in spelling and grammar checkers.

Another method to improve the quality of your content is to receive feedback from someone who is more knowledgeable on the subject matter (e.g., your professor or their teaching assistant). Because, as the saying goes, "You don't know what you don't know." Thus, when you lack experience on a subject, it becomes easy to overlook things that would be obvious to someone more experienced. This is one reason professors hold office hours, as they know you could use their assistance. In addition, some professors will require preliminary reports; take these seriously. Make sure your objective, methodology, and overall thought process is clearly laid-out in detail. These preliminary reports provide a great opportunity to improve the quality of your research and final paper. They allow the professor to point out any flaws or to relay if your overall scope of work appears too ambitious, or not ambitious enough, for the allotted time you're given to complete the project. Receiving this type of feedback is probably the most important feedback to earning a good grade. Because, almost regardless of your writing skills, your grade will suffer heavily if your research lacks important steps, if the overall scope of work is too small, or if your objective doesn't align with concepts taught in that class. (In other words, don't do a project on aerodynamics for a class on structural engineering.) If your professor doesn't require a preliminary report, go to their office hours (or write an email) to communicate your objective, methodology, and overall thought process. Note that the email route is not preferred since it can be challenging to be concise, but yet, still relay enough information to make your approach and goals clear. In contrast, speaking face-to-face allows for an easy back and forth dialogue. Another benefit of communicating with your professor is that you're showing effort. Teachers and professors love students that give effort and often will reward them for it. This can include bumping up your grade on the paper, or occasionally, increasing your final grade for the class. Now to be clear, they won't bump up your final grade much, but this can be the difference between a B+ and an A-.

If, for some reason, you can't receive feedback from someone with more experience, don't be afraid to ask another student. They may not know more than you, perhaps even less, but they can point out any glaring mistakes that we as humans tend to make on occasion. Note, though, that you should try to be conservative with the information you share with another student (assuming they're in the same class). Keep the conversation short and very high level. This, obviously, limits the amount of help they can give but is done out of an abundance of caution, and helps avoid any chance of copying (regardless of if it's accidental or intentional).

Lastly, I wanted to comment on the use of e.g. and i.e. Using them is optional, but they are a preference of mine since they provide a great opportunity to give more detail in a concise manner. If you do incorporate them, make sure you use them correctly. E.g. is an abbreviation for *exempli gratia*. This is a Latin phrase meaning "for example." A good way for us English speakers to remember this is to assume it's an abbreviation for "Example Given." On the other hand, i.e. derives from the Latin term *id est* and means "that is to say." Here, you can pretend i.e. is an abbreviation for "In Essence." Although, I remember it by the "i" alone, and think of the "i" as standing for "In other words." But, as always, use whatever trick works best for you. Here's an example of both in action:

1. After work, I like to go to a restaurant for dinner (e.g., Justin's Fine Dining or Rittenhouse's Steak House).

2. We need to start going to the gym regularly, i.e., to lose weight.

Chapter Bullet Points

- Your writing ability may be weaker than you think

- Even as a STEM major, it's important to write well

- Writing is a skill, and like any skill, it takes a conscious effort to improve

Notes

8. Understanding our limitations

8.1. Your own limits

Perhaps the most important lesson I learned throughout college was to understand the limits of my own knowledge. This concept was briefly discussed in Chapter 6, but it will be discussed more here, because this is an important topic and because there is an endless amount of information that exists and many fail to grasp the concept of limits to knowledge. For example, it is often cliché to say, "That person knows everything about X." Regardless of what X is (cars, finite element, Python, etc.), no one knows everything about it, and there is always more to learn. A more accurate statement would be, "That person knows far more about X than anyone in this room." Because, in addition to there always being more to learn, being an expert in anything is often relative to the people in the room. (Note: Of course, two or more experts can be in the same room.) For example, a group of non-engineers may call an entry-level engineer an expert on topics relevant to engineering. However, place that same engineer in a room with more seasoned engineers, and almost certainly, no one in that room would consider that entry-level engineer an expert.

I want to be clear. I am, by no means, trying to discourage anyone from learning; in fact, I am trying to do the opposite. Once you understand your limits, you'll stop settling and start digging deeper in your areas of interest, and eventually you will become an expert in your field. Though, after you greatly increase your knowledge on a subject, you won't feel like an expert. This is because the light bulb will have gone off, and you will finally understand that the amount of knowledge in this world is endless, even on a single topic. I promise, the Dunning-Kruger effect is real.

This lack of knowledge is one of the reasons I do believe attending college is a good idea (when done correctly). In risk management, you have unidentified risks called unknown unknowns. This means, you simply don't know what you don't know. It can be difficult, if not impossible, to research or fill in gaps in your knowledge that you simply don't know exist. Thus, a great way to reduce unknown unknowns is by reaching out to someone with experience – i.e., have someone teach you your unknown unknowns. Hence, this is why college is important. Unfortunately, an undergraduate degree does not make you an expert in anything. However, it will greatly reduce your unknown unknowns on topics relevant to your major and turn them into one of the other three categories in risk management: known knowns, known unknowns, or unknown knowns. All of which are better than unknown unknowns.

Of course, people will say, "A better and cheaper alternative to college is just reading a few books on a topic to learn everything you want to know." Undeniably, there is some truth within that statement; after all, most classes are taught from books anyway. However, I'll be blunt: This approach will not work in most cases, particularly if your goal is to become an expert and earn a good salary with a good job. I hate to be redundant from Chapter 2, but I will touch again on why I recommend that most people obtain at least a bachelor's degree. For better or worse, employers love college degrees, or at least, some form of certification showing you know something. If you're self-taught, it can be difficult to demonstrate to a hiring manager that you know what you claim to know. Thus, why would they hire a non-college educated engineer when the market is saturated with people who have a traditional four-year engineering degree? In most cases, it simply is not worth the risk. Fair or not, that is the reality. That said, never stop teaching yourself; a continuous learning attitude will take you far in life. A bachelor's degree is a door opener. The rest of your career journey depends on your willingness to keep growing and learning.

8.2. Limitations of the tools we use

8.2.1. Computer-aided numerical analysis tools

Computers are commonly used to solve complex problems, and a couple of tools frequently used by engineers include Finite Element Analysis (FEA) and Computational Fluid Dynamics (CFD). FEA is highly universal and frequently used to analyze stresses, displacements, and heat transfer. CFD is used to solve fluid flow problems (e.g., water flowing around a submarine or air flowing around a car). These are fantastic methods, and they have a proven track record of producing accurate approximations. However, the issue comes when young/future engineers start learning these programs (or other numerical methods). They believe these programs are magical black boxes; basically, they believe that they can just enter a couple of inputs and poof the results will be accurate. This issue is only getting amplified as these programs are becoming far too user-friendly. They allow the user to not truly understand what is actually happening. This is dangerous, and why I found it necessary to at least touch on the topic, even though this is a more advanced topic. But when you reach the stage in your education where you begin using computer-aided engineering programs, let's hope this book comes to mind. When using these programs, please do your homework and buy a book or two on the topic. Try to understand what is happening "under the hood" of these programs – i.e., what is the computer code doing? At the bare minimum, you need to be able to answer:

1. What governing equations are being used and why?

2. What assumptions are being used and why?

While it is important to know more, those two questions are common questions that young engineers can't answer. And if you can't answer those, you shouldn't trust your results. Additionally, understanding assumptions involves more than just understanding what assumptions are being made to solve the problem (e.g., steady-state for heat transfer). It also involves recognizing the program may make assumptions to set up the problem (e.g., contact surfaces or boundary conditions). However, the program doesn't know what you need to do; it can only perform the tasks you specify, or it may make guesses. Therefore, do not rely on default settings, and many of the automated steps should be checked manually (e.g., mechanical properties, boundary conditions, and contact surfaces). After you run a computer-aided engineering program, you need to analyze the results. Do the results make sense intuitively? If not, why not? Do the results line up with your hand calculations, results from a literature review, or laboratory testing? Note that complex problems are typically broken up into simpler problems, where "hand" calculations can be easily calculated to compare simulated results against. (These "hand" calculations can be done on a computer through writing code yourself.)

To reiterate, this book is not designed to teach you these programs, and it only covers the bare minimum that generally applies universally to computer-aided numerical methods programs. Thus, far more work is left up to the reader to learn more about each individual program before their computer-generated results can be trusted, as you don't want to produce results similar to the Sleipner A disaster. The Sleipner A, an offshore platform for oil and gas, sprang a leak in the concrete base and sank. Afterwards, an investigation revealed the finite element approximations were inaccurate, leading to an underestimation of shear stresses by 47%.[48] In nontechnical terms, certain concrete walls needed to be thicker. The Sleipner A disaster is far from an isolated incident, as numerical method errors have surfaced and caused destruction throughout history.

8.3. Limitations of your approach

Often, due to the inherent difficulties of the real world, we in the STEM field make assumptions. This is a great way to simplify a problem and make it easier to solve; however, it is important to understand why you made the assumptions. Students can fail to realize how and why a given assumption is ok to use. Thus, they can end up using an assumption to solve problems where the assumption is not valid. In class, that's ok, as the only harm is to your grade. In the real world, however, that is not ok. It could be costly, not just monetarily either: It could cause injuries or even death. A great example of an assumption engineers commonly make comes when they use gravitational acceleration. For practical purposes, we take gravitational acceleration as a constant, at 9.81 m/s^2 (or 32.2 ft/s^2) on earth. Although, this is not always the case. To demonstrate, let's look at the equation from which 9.81 m/s^2 is calculated:

$$g = G\frac{M}{r^2} \qquad\qquad (8.1)$$

g : Gravitational acceleration

G : Gravitational constant

M : Planet mass

r : Distance between two masses

It should be clear from the equation that gravitational acceleration is dependent on the distance between two objects. Thus, how could gravitational acceleration be a constant? It couldn't. However, because the distance to the center of the earth is so large, 3,959 miles (6,371 kilometers), the calculated change in the gravitational acceleration is negligible for many engineering problems.[49] In layman's terms, if an object is on the earth's surface or 1000 feet above the earth's surface, the difference in radius for the above equation is only 0.00478%, therefore, negligible for many problems.

At this point, you're probably wondering, "But aren't astronauts weightless in orbit? With the Earth being so large, surely gravity would still reach the International Space Station (ISS)?" Well, the ISS's altitude changes but is – approximately – 249 miles (400 kilometers) above the earth's surface.[50] At this altitude, gravity is nearly 89% of that on the earth's surface. To truly be weightless (i.e., avoid gravity), an astronaut would have to be a great distance from any other object in space. The perception of weightlessness in space that we typically see is due to the balance of the two main forces acting on the object (e.g., astronauts) in orbit, gravitational force (pulling the object "down") and the centrifugal force (pushing the object "out"). Basically, the object is in a constant state of free fall.

Nonetheless, the importance of understanding how universal constants are calculated should be clear. For example, so you don't accidentally use 9.81 m/s^2 for gravitational acceleration on the rare occasion when your problem requires a higher degree of accuracy. In college, professors often require you to write out the equation or, even worse, derive it from scratch rather than simply using a well-known constant or formula. You will hate it, especially if you're asked to do so on an exam; I know I did. However, I hope this section helps to ice the pain a little as there is a reason for the madness. Deriving an equation, or at least knowing how a universal constant is calculated, truly helps you understand when and how to use it.

To really drive home the point, let's talk about one of the most popular equations of all time, $f = ma$ (where f is force, m is mass, and a is acceleration). If you're an aerospace or mechanical engineering major, you'll use this equation a lot and probably far more than any other equation. Though, does f actually equal ma? Yes, of course it does, that's why we use it. However, does f ALWAYS equal ma? No, there is an underlying assumption being used to get f to equal ma. To know what this assumption is, you need to know were the equation derives from. In this case, it derives from Newton's Second Law which states force is equal to the change of momentum per change in time. In equation form, this equates to: $f = \frac{d(mv)}{dt}$ (where f is force, m is mass, v is velocity, and t is time). Thus, one must account for changes in BOTH, mass and velocity, with respect to time. But since mass often doesn't change with respect to time (i.e., is a constant), or if it does, the change is small enough to be negligible, we can simply use $f = ma$. Of course, one should note that acceleration is nothing more than the time derivative of velocity, $a = \frac{dv}{dt}$.

In layman's terms, acceleration equals a change in velocity with respect to a change in time – i.e., if you're going faster than you were a second ago, you had to accelerate. Long story short, I hope you fully grasp the importance of knowing where an equation derives from. You probably don't need me to tell you this, but there are real-world problems where the mass of an object does change with respect to time. Consequently, in those scenarios, you're probably going to have a real bad time if you use $f = ma$.

Chapter Bullet Points

- There is ALWAYS more to learn

- Computers are not magical black boxes; avoid treating them as such when using computer-aided numerical analysis tools

- Understand the assumptions you're making when using an equation or constant

Notes

9. Improve yourself

Now that we understand some of our limitations, let's try to reduce them. A good place to start is by creating good habits. Remember though, habits take time to form. If you're not used to doing something, such as homework, at first it will be tough to get motivated. But if you create a homework schedule, the same time every week (e.g., every Tuesday and Thursday from 5:00 p.m. to 8:30 p.m.), this schedule will become a habit. My old habit included working on schoolwork every Tuesday and Thursday from 4:30 p.m. to 8:00 p.m. I leave work at 4:00 p.m. Then I head straight to a local coffee shop and leave when they close. Notice I didn't head home. There are too many distractions at home, and it's far too easy to become sidetracked. Note though, if you have to work at home, for whatever reason (kids, weather, etc.), you need to create a defined workspace. A home office is ideal, but the main goal is to not be sitting on the couch watching TV while you "work." Work and play should be separated. If you don't have a home office, put a desk in the corner of your bedroom. If you're at that desk, it means the TV in the room has to be off and the door must be shut. Basically, do the best you can to remove as many potential distractions from your work area that your circumstances will allow. If you have the luxury of not doing schoolwork at home, remember to bring all your school supplies with you when you leave in the morning. Going home, even for a moment to grab your bag or food, is at best a waste of valuable time. At worst, you'll end up staying home for the night because you didn't feel like going back out. I know from experience that the latter happens far too often.

That said, remember that the best places for schoolwork will leave you with only two options: work or be bored. That is, the place you select shouldn't have fun distractions. They will, however, still have some distractions (e.g., noise levels at coffee shops). This is especially true on nights when there is a group that seems to think everyone should be listening to their conversation. This is unfortunate, but there are ways of reducing or even eliminating these distractions. Personally, I put my headphones in, and most days that is enough to drown out the noise. If my schoolwork requires reading or deep thought, instead of having music playing, I'll listen to pink noise, as I discussed in Chapter 6. Try it, it works! It's a nice soothing sound that doesn't distract you with words, but still works well to drown out the noises around you.

I will also add that you may have to work on school more than your scheduled days, like I did. Tuesday and Thursday were my "must" do schoolwork days, not my "should" do schoolwork days. As Tony Robbins says, there is definitely a difference in your mindset when it comes to the words "must" and "should." I find myself skipping far too many "I should do homework today" days, but I almost never miss a "I must do homework today" day. Because with the word "must" there are no ifs, ands, or buts about it, you have to do it. With the word "should" it becomes far too easy to say, "I should do schoolwork today, but my friends are at the lake, so I'll do it later." We have all been there; sometimes a nice beach day in the middle of August is simply too irresistible, even when you "should" be doing schoolwork. In summary, make sure you have "must" do schoolwork days in your schedule and fit in the "should" do schoolwork days when it is more convenient.

> "The difference between 'must' and 'should' is the life
> you want and the life you have." - Tony Robbins[51]

To build on that, make sure you have a schedule with routines that put you on track to reach your goals. Without routines, your goals may never come to fruition. Plus, they provide numerous other benefits, such as improving focus, reducing stress, reducing forgetfulness, increasing productivity, and improving confidence. These advantages can also be observed in businesses. For instance, A study performed on Gap employees took their normal unstable schedules (i.e., schedules that vary day-to-day) and stabilized them. As a result, sales increased by 7% and productivity increased by 5%.[52] These percentages may not seem overwhelming, but remember that Gap is a fairly large corporation. And in large corporations, because they have spent significant resources trying to optimize and increase profits for so long, it can be challenging to increase productivity by even a percent or two. Therefore, a 5% swing is a big deal. Moreover, Gap employees actually had schedules; all the researchers did was stabilize them. So ask yourself this, "If I go from having no schoolwork schedule to a stabilized schedule, how much will my productivity increase?" My guess is a whole lot more than 5%. Ultimately though, that's up to you to decide, but doesn't getting your schoolwork done early and in LESS time sound amazing? Well, that's the power of a set schedule with routines.

To assist you in creating a schedule, consider the following tips. First, remember Parkinson's Law from Chapter 6, which states work will expand to fill the time allotted for completion. This means, if you have homework due Monday morning, and you give yourself until Monday to complete the homework, we both know you're finishing that homework Sunday night (and you probably won't start until then either). On the other hand, if you give yourself until Friday morning, and assuming you have the willpower to hold yourself accountable, we both know you're finishing the homework Thursday night. Therefore, just because your professor says the homework is due in a week, doesn't mean your homework has to be due in a week. You can always set your homework "due" date earlier. Plus, the sooner you complete the homework, the sooner you can stop having it weigh on the back of your mind. Moreover, be mindful when allocating time for a task. Allocating extra time is fine, so you have ample time to complete the task without rushing, as rushing can cause you to make unnecessary mistakes. However, allocating too much time will lead to performing trivial matters, such as over-thinking insignificant details or, far worse, checking your social media accounts. For example, if you have a rough idea that homework in a certain class usually takes you an hour to complete, sure, go ahead and allocate two hours. But don't allocate three, four, or even more hours to complete it. You can always leave "early" once the homework is done, but leaving after three hours on a task that should take one hour isn't leaving early, even if you did schedule a four-hour time slot. Of course, some tasks can sometimes take much longer than expected. In this case, you can always stay late if your schedule allows. If not, and assuming you were wise enough to schedule the task early, you can always finish up another day. To put it simply, creating a schedule is not an exact science but at least be mindful of Parkinson's Law, so you can limit wasting your most valuable asset: time.

Next, be mindful of ego depletion, the concept that you have a limited amount of willpower. Yes, some research may have disproved this concept, as the study only observed ego depletion in people who actually believed you have a limited amount of willpower, while people who didn't believe willpower is limited, showed no signs of ego depletion.[53] Nevertheless, I think it's real, at least to some degree. Of course, given a tight deadline or other reasons a task needs to be done ASAP, I can rely on willpower to push through. That said, if I do have wiggle room to do the task a different day, and I've been working on tasks all day, and the task that has to be completed is challenging, then I'm far more likely to push it until another day. On the other hand, if the task is easy, I can normally muster up enough willpower to knock it out that night. I strongly assume I'm not alone in this. Hence, this is why ego depletion is important to account for when creating a schedule, despite what some research suggests. Thus, I try to knock out challenging tasks first. Then save the fun and/or easy tasks for later.

Furthermore, remember that your schedule is flexible, especially when starting a new one. If after the first week you don't like something, change it. Change your schedule to what makes you happiest while also allowing enough time to accomplish the tasks needed to meet your goals. Then once you have a schedule that fits you best, lock it in. Use it as a tool to hold you accountable. Thus, it should almost force you to actually work and complete tasks. Of course, if circumstances do change, your schedule can too. It's never completely etched in stone.

Let's revisit our discussion on habits. I find habits only take a few weeks to form and become a part of my normal routine. However, if it takes you longer, that's fine but stay consistent. One study suggests habits take 18 to 254 days to develop, with the average being 66 days.[54] Thus, eventually, things you don't enjoy doing, perhaps even despised doing, such as homework, will just become your normal routine. And, at that point, if you stopped doing that part of your routine (e.g., homework every Tuesday night), it will actually feel weird. With that said, remember that you should avoid skipping parts of a schedule as much as possible. Unfortunately, I know from experience that some schedules can be extremely fragile and are far too easy to break. Moreover, once broken, the painstaking part of redeveloping that habit starts all over. To build on that, remember to create a schedule that is easier for you to stick to. You do not have to make yourself miserable to achieve success. For example, I tried repeatedly to get up at 5:00 a.m. to work out before work. Eventually, I did form a habit and was able to do it for a little bit. But I was miserable and for the first half of my workout I was lethargic, which kind of defeats the purpose. Then once holidays came and I had a little bit of time off, I fell out of that habit. Honestly, I don't feel like getting it back. I don't like waking up at 5:00 a.m., nor do I like going to bed at 8:30 p.m. to ensure I get my eight hours of sleep. (Eight hours of sleep is a nonnegotiable part of my routine and it should be for you, too.) Now I work out after work, and it's significantly easier and better for me. I have energy during my workouts, and I'm not miserable all the time thinking about how early I have to go to bed and wake up. Long story short, try different schedules and create a routine that is easier for you to maintain. And just know, those motivational speakers that say you have to wake up at 4:00 a.m. to be successful in life are full of baloney. While there are benefits to waking up early, there are also benefits to staying up late. At the end of the day, we all get twenty-four hours, and there is no magic formula that will change that. Thus, adjust your schedule and routines to help you be the most productive you, you can be.

Also remember, you don't have to do any of this alone, and a good support system can be beneficial. If you have ever played sports, think of homework like practice. How often did you skip practice?

Probably nowhere near as often as you skip (delay) homework. Why? Partly because it was a habit. The other part is other people relied on you and held you accountable. Thus, don't be afraid to do homework in groups. Although, do not divide and conquer the homework. Every person in the group must do each problem. In addition, don't turn homework into a talking contest. When I did homework with other people, often I still had my headphones and so did they. Even in groups, the focus still needs to be homework. If there are people who won't stop talking, you just need to let them know, politely, that you need to focus. If they still talk a lot, unfortunately, you may have to exclude them from future homework sessions. Fortunately, if you're a STEM major, there should be plenty of students willing to meet up and knock out homework. Another bonus of group homework sessions is the opportunity to ask for help. Of course, you should attempt all the problems yourself (real attempts, not just a five-second attempt before asking for help), as you learn because of the struggles. The more you struggle, the more you learn. But if you really are stuck, having a friend there to help can be beneficial.

Regarding struggling, one of the best ways to improve your skills is by challenging yourself with unique projects. Don't be afraid to tackle exceedingly challenging projects, especially if you're truly passionate about them, projects so hard you don't even know where to begin. You need to try, you need to fail, and you need to try again and again. These failures are nothing more than fantastic learning opportunities. Remember, failure does not have to be the end result. Saying you "failed" is often just another way of saying you "quit."

"People don't fail, they quit." – Unknown

These projects can include school projects, too. Although, when it comes to school projects, make sure your professor is onboard, and you present them with a clear scope of work. In addition to school projects, it's beneficial to work on your own projects as well. Before you begin any project, ask yourself the following questions: What matters to you? What sparks your interest? What kind of work feels less like work and more like something you genuinely enjoy? Ideally, you answer these questions before starting a project so that you can align the project's goals with your future career goals.

Additionally, working on your own project will be better for you and more rewarding than watching endless TV all summer. Plus, if you do well, doing your own project will look great on a resume, far better than a school project of similar quality. It shows future employers (and/or colleges) that you have an enormous level of initiative, and that you're not afraid of hard work. Moreover, don't stress about not knowing how to start the project; once you research and think about the topic more, you'll figure out how to get started. But don't forget to start, that's the hardest part.

Unfortunately, far too often people won't even start a challenging project because it seems far too daunting. Here's the secret: All extremely challenging projects are done piece by piece, little by little. Additionally, the quality of your work will probably improve if you break up the project into smaller pieces. I find that I'm more willing to take the extra time to do a better job, especially on tasks that require significant time, when I break them up instead of trying to tackle everything at once. Building on that, understand that you don't need to see the entire path of a project (i.e., you don't need to know how to complete every step before you begin). If you can, the project isn't challenging enough. It should require you to learn skills and techniques you currently don't have. It should require thought to overcome challenging aspects. All you truly need is a goal, a willingness to learn, and the initiative to start. The rest will come together through hard work.

For example, think of the International Space Station (ISS). Former President Ronald Reagan directed NASA to build the ISS on January 25, 1984. But the first piece did not launch into space until 1998.[55] With how long it took, do you think the engineers tasked with designing the ISS had a clear path laid out in front of them? Do you think they knew exactly how they were going to pull off this monumental feat? I doubt they knew either; they simply had an end goal that had to be accomplished. The path to complete this goal was created one baby step at a time through endless R&D and continuous learning. Truth be told, sometimes it's best not to know all the hard work that is required beforehand as you may talk yourself out of it. For instance, this book has been far more daunting of a task than I could have ever imagined. If I knew that beforehand, I'm almost certain I would have talked myself out of it. So remember, often in life you need to just start doing and stop overthinking!

> "Most complex things in life are nothing more than small, simple things stacked together." – Justin Rittenhouse

And don't worry if the first iteration of your project isn't perfect or even very good. In fact, it probably won't be. Thankfully, the next iteration will be better with the knowledge you gain from the first iteration. The third iteration will be better yet. Even billion-dollar companies can't make a perfect product, as products are being improved all the time, with smartphones being a great example of this. They release a new and improved version every year, but this latest version simply wouldn't exist if not for all the hard work and R&D that went into the previous iterations. There is a word for this, kaizen, which means continuous improvement. Thus, remember to maintain a kaizen mindset for all of your projects. No matter how good (or bad) your project is, there is always room for improvement. In fact, sometimes you may even take a step backwards, and that's okay too, as you often won't know an idea doesn't work until you try it.

Moreover, never worry if you're smart enough to tackle a project, because you're as smart as any brain surgeon or rocket scientist out there. What, you don't think so? A study took 329 aerospace engineers and 72 neurosurgeons and evaluated several aspects of their cognition relative to the general population (18,427 other adults).[56] There were six domains in total: semantic problem solving, manipulation and attention, memory, spatial problem solving, problem solving speed, and memory recall speed. Aerospace engineers displayed no significant differences relative to the general population. Neurosurgeons did display a significant improvement for problem solving speed; however, they scored significantly worse with regard to memory recall speed than the general population. No significant differences were found between neurosurgeons and the general population for the other four domains.

Admittedly, sometimes it can feel like people are smarter. For example, they may figure out homework problems quicker. Nevertheless, don't be discouraged. You don't know what past experiences shaped them to develop these skills. Is the homework set math related? Maybe one of their parents is a math teacher, or maybe they spend far more time studying the material on their own than they admit to. Regardless, there is nothing stopping you from putting in more time until the homework becomes as easy for you as it is for them, perhaps even easier. It took me a long time to realize being smart is not a trait someone is born with, but is nothing more than a skill someone hones and develops through hard work.

A great example of this is the Polgár sisters. Their father, László

Polgár, was a researcher who wanted to prove intelligence is earned through hard work and isn't a trait someone is born with.[57] To prove this, he had a goal to have children and turn them into chess prodigies. He chose chess, even though he was a mediocre chess player, because the ranking system is well defined. Thus, if his children ranked high, there is little to no debating their skill. This is unlike other measuring sticks that are subjective, like writing, where people can debate all day long who the best writer is or even if a writer is actually good. Anyhow, László did end up having three daughters and exposed them to chess at very young ages. He did everything in his power to make sure they became elite chess players. The first daughter, Susan Polgár, at 15 became the top-ranked female chess player in the world. She was also the first woman to win the Chess triple crown and qualify for the Men's World Championship. Eventually, she even earned the title of grandmaster. Therefore, I would say that was a success, and he wasn't done yet. His second daughter, Sofia Polgár, at the age of 14 entered a tournament in Rome against several grandmasters. She won. She never did reach the same heights as her sister, but she did become the sixth best female chess player in the world. This means László was two for two in his quest to prove intelligence is earned through hard work. But, what about his third daughter? Well, she, Judit Polgár, became the best of the bunch. She became the fastest chess player ever to earn the title of grandmaster (including men) at just 15 years and 4 months old, and the youngest player to break the top 100 at only 12 years old. She is widely considered the best female chess player of all time. That's three for three.

Of course, there are obvious flaws within this experiment that should be acknowledged. For example, while a sample size of three is far better than one, it's still a rather small sample. Furthermore, a more scientific study would include control groups and multiple sets of parents. Regardless of these flaws, the results are astonishing. Oh, and if you're wondering why one sister is better than the next, they admit their skill level is a direct correlation to the amount of effort they put into training. (I.e., Judit put in the most effort, followed by Susan, then Sofia.) I won't comment on the ethical or moral aspects of performing experiments on your own children, but regardless, he did a fantastic job proving his point. Being smart is earned through hard work and not by the luck of the draw (i.e., not by something you're born with). I hope their story helps ingrain in you that you are capable of achieving anything. The only question is, are you willing to put in the work?

In addition to intelligence being a skill (i.e., something you can develop), it's also relative as no one is intelligent across all topics. It took me a long time to realize that, too. For example, if you need someone to rebuild your transmission, the world's best brain surgeon would probably be a pretty poor choice. Basically, we all have our nuggets of knowledge. Some people hone and develop their knowledge in fields such as mathematics or science while others choose areas such as cars or woodworking. Some even choose the jack of all trades route and try to gain knowledge across many fields. However, please note that those who are jack of all trades typically know basic concepts but lack a deeper understanding of their respective fields. They know enough to get by and, perhaps, enough to sound highly intelligent on topics if the room is full of people who lack the proper background. Nevertheless, if they end up talking to someone with a more in-depth background on a given topic, it can often become very apparent how little they know on said topic.

Honestly, the previous statement about sounding highly intelligent on topics if the room is full of people who lack the proper background can often be how teaching works. The students have either never seen the material or are still in the process of learning the material. Thus, they lack the proper background. This comes in handy as a teacher because not only are there lectures where teachers do not feel entirely comfortable with the material, but they will inevitably be tasked with teaching whole classes where they have little to no background. (At least college professors have to teach such classes.) I have been there myself; it's not fun, but if you prepare (study) for lectures, you will be fine. If you're curious about the frequency with which professors teach such classes, just know it is a common occurrence. In fact, there is literally a book called *Teaching What You Don't Know*.

With that said, it's worth acknowledging that most university professors do have PhDs, but even those with PhDs are, obviously, nothing more than human; an old saying that aptly captures this truth is "PhDs know a lot about a little." This means, they know a plethora of information about their research field, but because their research is so specialized, it is typically a narrow scope of knowledge. And outside of their field of research, they often have no more or less knowledge than anyone else. Truth be told, even within their respective fields, people with PhDs will always have infinitely more to learn. I remember when I took calculus, and my teacher, Mr. Drake, drew four circles on the board as seen in the following figures. The circles themselves represented the entire mathematical domain, and the filled-in portion represented Mr. Drake's self-perceived knowledge in the field of mathematics. The first circle was about half full, and Mr. Drake said after high school, he thought he knew about half of all the math that exists. After undergrad, Mr. Drake knew he expanded his knowledge of mathematics but understood there was still more to learn; hence, the second circle was about $\frac{2}{3}$ of the way full.

Mr. Drake also earned a Master's degree (actually two, I believe); this time, however, he finally understood the field of mathematics is far deeper than he originally thought or could have even comprehended. As a result, the third circle was only filled about $\frac{1}{4}$ of the way. Finally, the fourth circle is filled with nothing more than a few cracks, and Mr. Drake said, "After teaching mathematics for 30 years, I finally understand I know nothing more than a few cracks in the realm that is mathematics." Now admittedly, I took calculus over a decade ago, so my memory is a little fuzzy, but that was the gist of his story. I believe his journey is one that we all take throughout our lives, and his story makes more and more sense to me with every passing day.

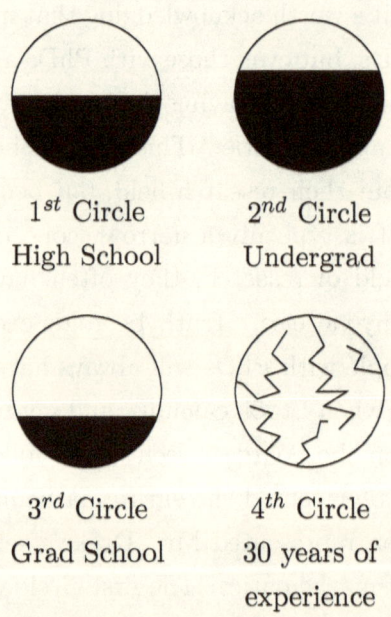

1st Circle
High School

2nd Circle
Undergrad

3rd Circle
Grad School

4th Circle
30 years of
experience

Long story short, we are all smart, and all of us are capable of anything. I know at times that can be hard to believe, but this is often nothing more than a self-confidence issue. This issue is true for me as well. Even though I have seen other people's work firsthand, as a professor, teaching assistant, and a fellow classmate, I still struggle with impostor syndrome to this day. I know firsthand my work is as good if not better than many of my peers, and I still struggle. But neither you nor I are alone, because a study released in 2011 found that an estimated 70% of people deal with impostor syndrome at some point in their lives.[58] While this percentage changes dramatically depending on the study you are reviewing (I think it's probably a lot higher), the point remains the same: If you think for a second you are alone in having self-doubts or feeling like a fraud, know you are far from alone. Truth be told, the struggle persists regardless of how many accolades someone accumulates. It gets better as you gain experience, but it never completely goes away. At least, it hasn't for me – not yet, anyway. In fact, I have a negative internal dialogue as I sit here writing these sentences. Trust me, I have thought about deleting this book many times, and pretending like I never wrote it. I definitely thought countless times that no one would ever read it, and if they did, they certainly wouldn't like it. That said, I know dreams are *not* achieved by sitting on the sidelines.

A source of self-doubt for students can often be other students, as some talk so confidently when discussing homework or how well they think they did on exams. They sometimes sound very convincing, almost as if they know the material better than the professor. All I would think during these discussions was, "Wow, they really know the material." Or I would think, "I thought I did that exam problem correctly, but that's not how I approached that problem at all. Thus, I probably got it wrong." It was not until graduate school that I started gaining confidence, mainly because I started working as a teaching assistant and learned firsthand that those "smart" kids, with all the confidence in the world (at least they projected themselves that way), earn bad grades, too. The more experience I gained as a teaching assistant, the more I realized we are all human. We all have classes that are more "natural" to us, and classes that we struggle in. Yes, even those kids who have a 4.0 GPA have classes they struggle in. They still get the A because they put in the work. They spend extra time on the homework; they go to office hours; and basically, they do what it takes to get the grade they want. But do not think for a second they don't struggle, because they do. Bottom line is this: Stop doubting yourself. You're a human, too. Anything someone else can do, you can do, too!

> "Your attitude, not your aptitude, will determine your altitude." – Zig Ziglar

Finally, an important aspect of growing intellectually is understanding the world is not black and white, right or wrong. Most reading this book are at the dualism stage of Perry's Stages of Cognitive Development. This is perfectly fine and a part of your natural development. As you progress through your educational journey, you should advance through his later stages. A brief breakdown of Perry's four major categories can be seen next; however, it is important to note that these categories are further subdivided into more detailed stages, and you should spend time reviewing the full breakdown. (Do a web search for "Perry's Stages of Cognitive Development.")

1. Dualism

   - Answers are right or wrong

2. Multiplicity

   - There are conflicting answers

3. Relativism

- A realization and acceptance that conflicting viewpoints can coexist, and that knowledge and beliefs are often context dependent

4. Commitment

    - You acknowledge that many viewpoints exist, and you now have the ability to analytically evaluate them. But, based on your experiences, you start recommitting to your beliefs and/or committing to new ones

9.1. Underlying concepts

The downfall for many students when it comes to exams is they fail to grasp the underlying concepts the homework was meant to establish. Far too often students believe exam questions are completely different than homework questions. This is typically not the case. The problem lies with students learning to solve a specific problem or solve problems in a specific way. This is usually caused by students rushing through the homework as fast as possible. Instead, students should take time after solving a homework problem and ask themselves, "Why did I use those equations?" and "What concepts should I have learned (e.g., required assumptions or relationships between variables)?" If students actually took the time to understand what they did and why they did it on the homework, similar problems on the exam wouldn't look so foreign. Also, when it's time to study for the exam, don't just practice the homework problems. Do those and make sure you understand those well, but then, do other problems out of the same section/chapter of the book. If you cannot solve these additional problems just as easily as the homework, you probably have not grasped the concepts the professor wanted as well as you think. The additional problems also provide opportunities for repetitive exposure to the material, which is helpful in combating memory loss. Memory loss is a known phenomenon that happens at an exponential rate; this is known as the forgetting curve.[59] Basically, after learning new information, you tend to forget up to 90% of it within a week (and 50% within one hour). Researchers suggest repetition over time and revisiting the same material serve as tools to help memory retention. Hence, why you should be reviewing your homework before the exam.

An additional reason you may not be grasping the material as well as you think is that you relied on the example problems in the book more than you realized. A good way to solve this issue is by solving the homework problems BEFORE reviewing the example problems. This approach is harder, but it does allow you to compare your method of solving the problem to the book's. And again, remember, you learn through the struggles. If you don't struggle, you don't learn (at least not anywhere near as much). Next are two examples to help illustrate the differences between homework and exam problems, and how understanding the underlying concepts in the homework can make the exam problems equivalent in difficulty to the homework problems.

Example #1

Homework Question: Justin weighs 849 N on Earth; what is his mass?

Required Governing Equation:

$$F = ma$$

Where F is force (weight is a force), m is mass, and a is acceleration. Rearranging the equation to solve for our unknown, mass:

$$m = \frac{F}{a}$$

Plugging in the numbers:

$$m = \frac{849 \ N}{9.81 \ \frac{m}{s^2}} = 86.5 \ kg$$

Note that for homework and exams it's standard to assume $9.81 \ \frac{m}{s^2}$ (or $32.2 \ \frac{ft}{s^2}$) as the gravitational acceleration on Earth, unless it's otherwise specified.

Exam Question: Justin, who has a mass of 86.5 kg, and his friends took a trip to the Sun to, of course, make s'mores. They traveled at a speed of $81 \ \frac{m}{s}$. And the Sun was hot that day at $5,505°C$, and the gravitational acceleration of the Sun is $274 \ \frac{m}{s^2}$. How much does Justin weigh on the Sun, assuming he can withstand the heat?

This question appears to be significantly harder than the homework, but is it? Ask yourself, how could this problem relate to the homework problem? It should be clear that a lot of the variables used are the same: weight, mass, and gravitational acceleration. Yes, the exam question has more variables, but those are just to throw you off. If the extra variables don't throw you off, you'll realize this problem is actually easier than the homework problem.

Required Governing Equation:

$$F = ma$$

Plugging in the numbers:

$$F = 86.5 \ kg * 274 \ \frac{m}{s^2} = 23,701 \ N$$

If you actually grasped the homework, I hope it's clear how easy the exam problem was. But admittedly, that was a pretty basic example and the exam problem didn't appear that different relative to the homework problem. Thus, let's try an example where the exam problem appears radically different.

Example #2

Homework Question: A box has a cross-sectional area of 1.5 m² and is tasked with holding an object that weighs 500 N. What is the engineering stress?

Required Governing Equation:

$$\sigma = \frac{F}{A}$$

Where σ is stress, F is force, and A is area.
Plugging in the numbers:

$$\sigma = \frac{500 \ N}{1.5 \ m^2} = 333.33 \ Pa \ (or \ \frac{N}{m^2})$$

Exam Question: A box has a length of 2 m, a width of 1.5 m, a height of 5 m, and a weight of 250 N. Justin, a human who is currently on Earth, stands on this box, and due to this, the box is subjected to an engineering stress of 283 Pa. If Justin has an awesome factor of, at least, ten times that of a normal human, what is his mass?

Before we get started, let's break this exam problem down in even more detail, and ask ourselves some questions.

1. What concepts did we learn via the homework problems?

   - Homework problem 1: We learned the relationship between force, mass, and acceleration.

   - Homework problem 2: We learned the relationship between stress, force, and area.

2. What governing equations did we use in the homework problems?

   - Homework problem 1: $F = ma$

   - Homework problem 2: $\sigma = \frac{F}{A}$

3. How do the first two questions apply here?

   - Well, what do we need to find? Mass.

   - Are there any equations we learn that can help us find mass? Yes, $F = ma$.

   - Can that equation be used here? It appears so, as we need to find m, and we know a equals 9.81 $\frac{m}{s^2}$ since the problem stated, "a human that is currently on Earth," but we don't know force.

   - Is there any other equation we learned from the homework problems that we can use to find the missing variable, force? Yes, $\sigma = \frac{F}{A}$.

   - Can that equation be used here? Yes, as we are given two of the three variables, stress and area, and the only one missing is the one we need, force. (Engineering students are expected to have the equations for the area of a circle, square, and rectangle memorized. These equations are

$A = \pi * radius^2$, $A = width^2$, and $A = length * width$, respectively.)

- There appears to be three variables that we don't need, the height of the box, the mass of the box, and Justin's awesome factor. Are we sure we don't need these? If so, why don't we?

  - Height plays a role in calculating the volume of the box or the vertical cross-sectional area. But since we don't need volume for our governing equation, and gravity causes you to stand on top of boxes rather than their sides, height does not play a role here.

  - The box having a weight of 250 N does not play a role because the question is asking us to calculate Justin's mass not the mass of the box. In addition, the question states, "the box is subjected to an engineering stress" caused by Justin standing on the box. Therefore, the question is implying Justin's weight is causing the stress.

  - Of course, the fact Justin is at least ten times as awesome as a normal human plays a very significant role, just not in this problem, for what I hope are obvious reasons.

Now since we answered those questions, we can get started.
Part one, find Justin's weight:
Required Governing Equation:

$$\sigma = \frac{F}{A}$$

Rearranging the equation to solve for our unknown, force:

$$F = \sigma * A$$

Plugging in the numbers:

$$F = 283 \; Pa * (1.5 \; m * 2 \; m) = 849 \; N$$

Part two, find Justin's mass:
Required Governing Equation:

$$F = ma$$

Rearranging the equation to solve for our unknown, mass:

$$m = \frac{F}{a}$$

Plugging in the numbers:

$$m = \frac{849 \; N}{9.81 \; \frac{m}{s^2}} = 86.5 \; kg$$

For this exam problem you actually had to use two homework questions to solve, but again, if you actually grasped and understood the homework problems, it should have been fairly straightforward. Extra variables, using multiple equations, or solving for a different variable from the same equation should not confuse you. If they do, then you don't actually understand the material. Thus, you should be doing additional homework problems. Just remember that the hard part of an engineering exam is just selecting the right equations, also known as the governing equations, for the problem. Once that is done, the problem will often become trivial to solve and nothing more than plug and chug.

Also, don't be afraid to double-check your work on exams if time permits. Instead of rushing to be the first one done during the exam, which adds zero value to your resume or future career, take the extra time to evaluate and perform sanity checks on your answers. Performing sanity checks could potentially boost your GPA, but the real value comes from developing the habit itself, which becomes an essential habit once you start working full time. Sanity checks can be as complicated as solving the problem using a secondary method, or as simple as thinking through the answer and asking yourself if it makes sense. For example, if you were asked to solve for the gravitational acceleration on the moon but calculated an answer higher than the gravitational acceleration on earth, that should be a red flag, and you should immediately know that the answer is incorrect – unless the professor used fictitious numbers. Either way, at that point, it would be wise to double-check all your calculations.

I also wanted to touch on exams where professors simply reword or change the numbers in homework problems and use them as exam problems. This method for creating an exam is okay, but it doesn't clearly illustrate that the students understand the underlying concepts. Exam problems should look different from homework problems, and they should make students think. When exam problems appear completely different, it helps the professor assess who understands the material well and who is simply good at copying and pasting (i.e., memorizing the homework problems). I know these thought-provoking questions can be frustrating, but just know professors are creating them because they care, not to annoy students. I know many of you, after taking such an exam, will say things like, "In the real world, we have more time to solve these problems," or

"In the real world, engineers work in groups." I know you'll say these things because I said them. But I was wrong, and you are too. While I do agree that you'll have more time to solve problems in the real world than on an exam, you still have time constraints. Projects have deadlines and unless you want to work eighty hours a week, I suggest you learn how to solve problems in a timely manner. Moreover, as far as working in groups goes, that simply isn't true. In fact, I have spent far more time solving engineering problems solo than in groups in industry. We may collaborate to discuss the overall project scope, but the underlying math and work is often done solo. In my experience, even when you do work together to solve a complex math problem, it's never in groups. Typically you both solve the problem separately, then come together to see if you got the same answer.

Furthermore, for those thinking, "It still isn't fair that professors try to 'trick' you with irrelevant information and useless variables," my question to you is, what do you think happens in the real world? I promise, there isn't someone handing you the exact variables and equations you need to solve a problem. Often, you are given nothing but the problem. For instance, instead of "Justin weighs 849 N on Earth, what is his mass?" your boss will say, "Go figure out Justin's mass." Of course, you can always ask follow up questions, such as "How much does Justin weigh?" Unfortunately, your boss doesn't always have the answer, and he'll just say, "I don't know, you have to figure it out." At this point, you have to determine the required equations and variables on your own in the real world, which has an endless amount of irrelevant information and useless variables, or, in some cases, not enough information. In that case, you have to determine how you can get the information and/or variables you need. Does the guy across the hall know? Does the person in the test lab know? Can you perform your own test to find the missing variable? If it's just not achievable to obtain that last variable, then what? Do you give up? (For the record, not being able to obtain a variable is common in the real world.) Often, if you're unable to obtain a variable, the best approach is to make a conservative estimate of its value, erring on the side of safety. For example, if you know the number has to be less than X, for one reason or another, then you may use $1.10 * X$, $2 * X$, or even over $10 * X$ as X, depending on the project and how safe you need to be.

For example, if you needed to know Justin's weight to build a stable box for him to stand on, and, perhaps, Justin is a very private person who doesn't want to share any information about himself, then what? Well, by looking at him one can reasonably conclude he clearly weighs less than 1150 N [258.5 lbs]. Therefore, in the real world you may use 2300 N [517.1 lbs] as his weight. (That is, here we used $2 * X$ as X.) This is far from an exact science, and picking 1150 N and a safety factor of two are, in some ways, arbitrary. Regardless, even with the missing variable, we were able to design a box that any reasonable person would call safe for Justin to stand on. And, in engineering, often that is all you can hope to do. I hope the point is clear by now, that no matter how hard you think an exam problem was, the real world can be much harder. I promise that engineers working in industry wish they were handed all the variables they needed when given a problem to solve. They probably won't even mind if someone throws in a couple of extra variables they don't need, as just having the variables they do need would make their lives a thousand times easier.

9.2. Seek assistance

First, know that there are other places, besides your professor or classmates, where you can go to receive help. Many universities have dedicated areas to assist students with their studies. This can include anything from tutoring for STEM homework to helping students write essays. The latter is incredibly helpful for students whose native language differs from that of their college. Thus, make sure to ask around and see what is available at your college. Also, make sure to ask more than one person (e.g., other students, librarians, or the receptionist for the college of engineering), as one person may not know of all the places students can go to receive help. The best part is these resources are often free, and in my experience, seldom used. Most of my tutoring hours came and went without a single student coming for help. This was also true for my office hours at WMU and MVNU. As a professor, it can be frustrating to see students struggling but never seeking help. To be clear, this is 100% on the students. They are adults now and need to take responsibility by seeking help when they need it. It is not on the professor to seek you out. Professors are incredibly busy, as they often have many students and teach multiple classes. They simply do not have time to follow up with every student, especially at larger schools. Consequently, don't be afraid to ask for help. No one expects you to know everything. There may be a time when a topic just won't click for you. At that point, go to office hours and ask for help. Professors are required to hold these for a reason. Colleges, their administration, and professors all fully understand learning something new can be challenging at times. Though, before taking advantage of office hours, make sure you're not being lazy. Imagine how busy a professor would be if every student went and asked a question every time they got stuck? I'm not sure there is enough time in the day for the professor to answer all of those questions. Therefore, not only should you attempt the problem before asking for help, but you need to take the attempt seriously. And no, five minutes is not a serious attempt, nor is only using your class notes or class book. You need to utilize other resources (e.g., online tutorials or other classmates). Some professors, as they should, may ask to see your attempts. If you didn't give adequate effort, they may ask you to go attempt the problem again before they will provide any help. This may seem harsh, and may make you mad, but it's the right approach. A professor that enables you to be lazy is not a good professor, regardless of how nice you think they are. They need to be preparing you for the working world. Once you enter industry, do you think your boss wants you asking a question every five seconds? I promise you, they don't. Long story short, if you are legitimately stuck, seek help.

It should be noted that using office hours doesn't just benefit you in the moment (i.e., you get help with that immediate problem); it could have long term benefits, too. It shows the professor you care and are putting in the effort to succeed. Many professors will notice and appreciate it. In fact, when it comes time for final grades, professors are more willing to round up if you have put in extra effort all semester long. The key phrase there is, "all semester long." If you were struggling and never once went to office hours, don't expect the professor to be too sympathetic at the end of the semester when you come asking if there is any way for you to increase your grade to avoid failing the class. You had all semester to seek help, and now you want to put in the effort? Sorry but it simply doesn't work that way. College is a marathon, not a sprint. You need to be putting in effort the whole semester. If you did, you probably wouldn't be in the position of failing the class. Thankfully, if you did show up to office hours and did put in the work, you'll find professors are typically more sympathetic. They may even give you an opportunity to improve your grade.

There is another source of help that is very easy to access: actually reading the feedback provided by your professors. Too many students look at the final grade on a report and then shove it in their bag. Professors spent time reading it and providing feedback to help you learn, so take the time to read their notes. This is also true for exams (or any other graded item). For items such as weekly lab reports, students will make the same mistakes repeatedly, and the professors are forced to provide the same feedback and, of course, markdown the report every single time. To cut to the chase, your grade will improve if you actually take the time to read all feedback provided by your professors.

Lastly, because this is a section on self-improvement, I just want to remind you to start believing in yourself. The sooner you fully grasp that we are all human – and that, no one, past or present, is more (or less) capable than you are – the sooner you can start working towards goals you never dreamt possible. In an effort to drive home this point, I'll end this chapter on a quote from one of my favorite motivational speakers, Les Brown. And for those who don't know him, and to give the quote even more context and meaning, just know Les Brown was born in an abandoned building and labeled educable mentally retarded in the fifth grade.

> "The easiest thing I ever did was earn a million dollars. The hardest thing I ever did, and it took years, was believing I was capable of earning a million dollars." – Les Brown

Chapter Bullet Points

- Remember to form good habits

- Consistently challenge yourself with hard projects

- Intelligence is a skill that can be developed

- Make sure you fully understand the concepts that your homework is meant to teach you

- Never be afraid to ask for help

- Stop doubting yourself; you're a human, and so is the next person; thus, you're just as capable

Notes

_____

_____

_____

_____

_____

_____

10. Reduce stress

College can be a highly stressful time for many. And while having some stress is actually a good thing, since it pushes you and can help you grow as a person, too much can be overwhelming. As a college student, you must find ways to manage your stress levels. Fortunately, a lot of stress is self-inflicted. Colleges have been around a long time, and for the most part, haven't changed much. Thus, there shouldn't be many surprises. You have classes, you have homework, you have projects, and you have exams. Rinse and repeat.

That said, one source of stress is facing difficult professors, but nowadays, tools such as RateMyProfessors.com can help ensure their difficulty level doesn't come as a surprise. It is important to note that you shouldn't make any rash judgments about professors based on online tools. These tools are limited for a number of reasons, such as limited sample size and the student's state of mind when leaving a review. Now to be clear, I have no evidence but would assume a person would leave a more negative review after failing a class than the professor probably deserves. Therefore, use online tools with more traditional resources such as your fellow classmates. If everything online says the professor is tough, and all your friends say the professor is tough, then the professor is probably tough. Sometimes the professor will even admit they are tough as a point of pride. Therefore, once you collect the information about the professor and realize they are tough, account for that when selecting classes. You have a few options here: 1) reduce your class load during the semester you take that professor's class; 2) rearrange your schedule to take easier classes during that semester; 3) if possible, take the class with a different professor; or 4) if the first three options aren't feasible or you prefer not to make any changes, acknowledge that the class will be challenging, and let your friends know that during that semester you'll have less free time.

Moreover, to reduce your stress, try to avoid taking on a course load larger than you can manage. It is far too common for students to try and rush through college. Students should try to remember that they, hopefully, have a long life ahead of them. If college takes you a year (or more) longer than your peers, does that really affect your long-term goals? Probably not. However, rushing through college will probably lead to a lower GPA, less long-term memory retention, and more stress. Thus, if your work-life balance only allows you to take two to three classes at a time, so be it.

Consequently, avoid judging your level of success based on others and, of course, don't judge other people's success. Everybody's situation is unique, and the level of someone's success cannot be solely measured based on what they have accomplished. Their personal path, goals, and other unknowns can be important variables that must be accounted for; although, they often aren't. Hypothetically, imagine two individuals: one raised in a broken home, working full-time throughout high school and college, and the other from a stable home with a supportive family providing both financial and emotional support throughout high school and college. If both individuals earned a bachelor's degree, which one is more impressive? I believe most would agree the individual from the broken home has a more impressive path. Now, how about if the person from the broken home took an extra year or two to complete the degree and had a slightly lower GPA? Again, most people would agree the path of the student from the broken home is more impressive. Similar logic can easily be applied to other variables such as unknown medical issues or different career goals.

Anyhow, I don't want to downplay the success of either individual from that example. They both had a goal, and both accomplished their goal of obtaining a college degree. Therefore, both deserve credit. Nevertheless, I hope the point here is clear: Never create self-inflicted stress comparing yourself to someone else. You never know someone's full story. Even if you think you do, you don't. Life is far too complex and perception can often be far from reality. Therefore, it is best to define your goals and create a path that aligns with those goals and not focus on someone else's success. Focus on you and your goals! Furthermore, never forget what Teddy Roosevelt once said:

"Comparison is the thief of joy." – Theodore Roosevelt

Homework is another added stressor for college students. One of the easier ways to reduce homework stress is to complete it early, when able. Admittedly, I was a procrastinator myself, and like many, thought the due date meant "due today." But whenever I did home-work early, I felt much better, as I didn't have it lingering in the back of my mind as something I still had to do. Waiting to do homework until the day it's due, or the night before, can add stress in a few ways. First, you suffer because you know you have to do it, and it just sits there in the back of your mind until it's complete. Secondly, if you allocate just enough time to complete the homework, and you get stuck on a problem, panic mode sets in. This can lead to a high level of stress which is completely unnecessary. Thus, I ask, why do it to yourself?

Another positive of doing homework early is that it could lead to a better grade, which could decrease your long-term stress levels. There are several reasons your grade may improve. You don't have to worry about running out of time. You avoid the need to submit an incomplete assignment. You have the freedom to think through problems without feeling rushed. If you can't solve a problem, you'll have time to seek help, and you'll also have the opportunity to experience that "Oh shoot, I did that wrong" moment before submitting your work. More than once, after turning in my homework, I had a "eureka" moment. Unfortunately, after handing it in, it is simply too late. (Yes, I, too, have had eureka moments after exams.) Just to be clear, I'm not saying allocate more time to homework as I fully understand time is a precious resource, and let's not forget about Parkinson's Law from Chapter 6. All I'm suggesting is to choose wisely when to allocate time for homework. It's better to allocate time closer to when homework is received than to when it's due. This allows for more flexibility if homework does not go as planned.

Being organized is another effective way to reduce your stress and help you complete homework in a timely manner. To start, create a schedule and be sure to include ample time for homework, as homework time is often forgotten by students. This is because the typical student will fit homework in when they are bored or when it's convenient. But you have a scheduled time for class, and you have a scheduled time for work, so why wouldn't you have a scheduled time for homework? Another benefit of having a scheduled homework time is it allows you to enjoy non-homework time even more, since it kind of gives you permission to not do homework and enjoy yourself outside of your scheduled homework time. I know before I had a scheduled homework time, regardless of what I was doing, I couldn't get the fact that I had homework to do from lingering in the back of my mind. But having a scheduled time definitely made my leisure time more fun and relaxing.

Planners are another way to improve your organization. It can be hard, if not impossible, to remember items such as due dates, meetings, or appointments. You don't have to use a paper planner, either; if you prefer, you can use a phone app to avoid adding another item to carry and remember. I regularly use the Notes, Reminder, and calendar applications on my phone to keep up with my busy schedule. It is astounding how much you forget when you don't write things down, especially with a busy schedule. I know some of you may think, "I don't need to write information down, I'll just remember it." You're wrong. While you might get by without writing things down, I promise you, you're forgetting more than you realize. This is only amplified as you gain responsibilities and your schedule gets busier. Using planners and/or phone applications also provides good practice before entering the working world. Other than some new employees, I don't know a single person who works in a college degree-required career who doesn't write down their to-dos in some form or another. A person with a truly busy schedule cannot and will not remember everything. It's time to set the ego aside and start writing things down. (And yes, all new employees learn over time that they have to write down information. Be ahead of the curve here, not behind.)

Another lesson all college students need to learn is to stop worrying over a bad grade. It happens. Most students do bad or even fail an exam at some point during their academic career, including me. Thus, I fully understand that not worrying is easier said than done. Nevertheless, it is important to remember that one failed exam, in all likelihood, will have zero effect on your career and may even have minimal impact on your grade in the class. If you work hard, you could still receive a good grade, perhaps even an A. Even if you don't receive a great grade in that class, it's still important to remember the world didn't come to an end and you're still alive.

To ease your mind and demonstrate that even a bad class grade is not the end of the world, let's do some math. It takes roughly 120 credits to earn a bachelor's degree. Let's pretend your school lets you completely fail a class without retaking it, meaning you now have a GPA of 0.0 for one class. (Note that schools typically make you retake failed classes until you earn a GPA of at least 1.0 or 2.0, depending on the class and school.) If you had a 4.0 in all other classes, the class you failed was a three credit course, and your degree required 120 credits, your final college GPA is still a 3.9. That is an outstanding GPA. The only thing that one bad grade did was stop you from graduating with a 4.0 (or the highest GPA possible on your school's scale).

As far as not having a 4.0 GPA goes, the truth is that I have applied for and seen many job postings in my lifetime, and I have yet to see one require a 4.0. The highest GPA requirement you'll probably ever see is 3.75, and that is extremely rare. I believe I have only seen a GPA requirement above 3.5 once. Most commonly, from my experience, when a GPA requirement is listed, the required GPA is "3.0 or above" (on a 4.0 scale). However, most often there is no GPA requirement. While a high GPA is a nice-to-have item on the resume, it is far from the most important item. As discussed in Chapter 5, experience is far more important. That is, the projects you've worked on and the real-world experience you have outweigh a high GPA. Truth be told, to my knowledge, every engineering student I graduated with was able to obtain a well-paying engineering job after college. Some took a little longer than others (talking months longer not years), but all were able to receive an offer sooner or later. This includes students with GPAs that were below 2.5. The truth is that GPAs rarely come up in interviews. After graduation and a few years of full-time experience, your GPA won't even matter. By then, it's all about the experience you've gained. For more information on high GPAs and their relevance, please refer back to Section 5.1. (Remember that you don't need to include your GPA on your resume if it's not high enough.)

Seeking out and receiving emotional support is another way to reduce stress. The most obvious way to find support is to have a family member or friend as a go-to for venting your frustrations. Similarly, for schoolwork, working in groups is another great option for reducing stress. Those within the group don't even have to be working on the same project or assignment. I, like many engineering students, have spent many all-nighters in a computer lab finishing up projects. And, it's just a good feeling to see another person pulling an all-nighter, too; misery loves company. Often, we wouldn't even talk. Every few hours we would look at each other, and the conversation would go as follows:

"This sucks, doesn't it?"
"Yup."

And then we would get back to work. It clearly isn't much, but even that is a nice little pick-me-up, as there's joy in simply knowing you're not alone. There are other people out there grinding and putting in the work just like you. While it's true that working alone on hard projects can potentially be more productive, and may need to be done from time to time, it's important to remember that people need other people. It's just the way we are wired. Don't get me wrong, I'm an introvert myself, and I'm not saying you need large groups of people. You can if you want, but I'm just saying you need some interaction to keep your morale high. This can be as little as one other person.

That said, there is no doubt that schoolwork can be tiring and wear you down. Thus, make sure to leave time in your schedule to pursue your passions, as it's important to have something in your schedule that brings you joy and excitement. This not only reduces stress but can also boost your self-esteem.

In addition to pursuing your passions, performing random acts of kindness can also boost your self-esteem and relieve stress. It is truly amazing how doing something for someone else can make YOUR day. It doesn't have to be big either, small acts of kindness can go a long way. It can be as little as buying lemonade from a child or anonymously paying for someone's meal.

One topic that many like to avoid, but can have a profound impact on both your stress level and overall happiness, is health. One way to improve your health and reduce stress is to eat well. A poor diet tends to be a terrible cycle of consuming more junk food for a sugar buzz, which quickly wears off, leaving you more tired than before (i.e., you crash). To counteract this, many turn to the popular drug known as caffeine. However, caffeine use should be limited or avoided altogether, which I know goes against the desires of most college students. While it's true caffeine can help wake you up, it can also intensify stressful situations.[60]

The best way to avoid both, junk food and caffeine, is to eliminate the need for a quick boost, and to achieve this, a well-rounded diet is an excellent place to start. (Note: We will touch on other methods later, such as sleep, exercising, and avoiding alcohol.) A healthy diet has been proven to reduce stress and give you a natural pick-me-up. For example, a study published in 2021 compared stress levels in participants whose daily intake of fruit and vegetables was at least 470 grams versus those with an intake of less than 230 grams.

Participants with the higher intake had a 10% reduction in stress levels.[61] Another 2021 study found that those who consume meat had lower levels of depression (Hedges' g = 0.216) and anxiety (g = 0.17) compared to those who abstained from eating meat.[62] In addition, a healthy diet can help you avoid weight-related stress. This includes potential health-related or self-image issues, as many are self conscious about excess weight. The good news is that the "freshman 15" appears to be a myth, with a 2008 study showing the average freshman gained only 2.7 lbs, though this is still almost six times the average weight gain for the general population over a six month period.[63] Thus, as you transition from high school to college, you need to be proactive in creating or maintaining a healthy lifestyle.

To complement a healthy diet, avoid drinking alcohol, as alcohol does not alleviate stress; it only masks it – temporarily. Thus, similar to junk food and caffeine, an unhealthy cycle tends to develop leaving you always wanting more. In addition, alcohol can influence the way your body perceives and responds to stress. This means a heavy drinker could experience higher levels of anxiety when confronted with a stressful event, compared to a nondrinker (or moderate drinker).[64]

Along with gaining control of your eating habits, remember to include exercising into your routine. I know with the endless amount of homework you have, it feels like you don't have time. But if something is important, you make the time, and exercising is that important. A workout program not only helps you feel and look good physically, but, more importantly, it can have a profound impact on your mental health. Exercising has been proven to increase your endorphins, reduce stress, and improve your mood. When it comes to exercising, do what you enjoy. Far too often I see people doing exercises they hate, and, more often than not, they don't stick with it. The goal is to get your heart rate up and to get moving. There are endless ways to make that happen, such as playing games (e.g., football, basketball, or tennis), kayaking, hiking, etc. You don't always have to lift weights or go to the gym. Though you should incorporate some weight lifting into your regimen, as a 2020 study revealed that participants who strength trained, either with weight lifting or bodyweight exercises, twice a week over an eight-week period, felt a 20% reduction in anxiousness and stress.[65]

When it comes to resistance training, if you decide to work out only twice a week, research push-pull and upper-lower splits, as either approach is fantastic. When doing your research, note that people often overexaggerate, and, regardless of what someone may say, there is no exercise that is a must, as many alternatives exist. With that said, there are exercises that many agree to be staples in a good workout program. The three most common are bench, squat, and deadlift, but other popular choices include pull-ups and military press. While these exercises don't have to be in your program, unless you have a reason to avoid them (e.g., previous or current injury), I would recommend including them. One aspect that makes these exercises great is that they are compound lifts, meaning they work multiple muscle groups. In most cases, you should be prioritizing compound movements over isolation movements (bicep curls, tricep pushdowns, etc.).

A few other important points to remember to ensure you're using your time in the gym efficiently include progressively overloading, consuming adequate high-quality protein, getting proper rest, and training close to failure or to failure. To progressively overload, track the amount of weight you used and the number of reps you completed for each exercise, or at least for your main compound lifts, using pen and paper or one of the many available apps. The goal is to constantly be trying to increase the weight or your rep count compared to your last workout.

With regard to eating adequate high-quality protein, the rule of thumb for the proper amount can vary widely depending on the source. Typically though, if you want to build muscle, it ranges between 0.6–1.0 grams of protein per pound of your ideal body weight. For example, if someone weighs 220 lbs, but their ideal weight is 190 lbs, and they want to aim for the middle at 0.8, they should try to consume 152 grams of protein a day. That said, I aim for 100–150 grams of protein per day. (I weigh between 190–200 lbs, on average.) Note: I do recommend doing your own research on the quantity and quality of the protein you consume since some argue for consuming less protein than the range I provided and all protein is NOT equal. Just because the nutritional facts list 10 grams of protein, it does not mean your body is using 10 grams of that food's protein. A great place to start your research on protein quality is knowing the Digestible Indispensable Amino Acid Score (DIAAS) of the food you are eating.

Moreover, remember that muscle is built during the rest and recovery phase and not the workout. The workout is required to stimulate growth, but overtraining will actually limit growth and strength potential. That being said, it's still important that you're lifting with intensity. Whether or not you should take every working set (non-warm-up sets) to failure is debatable, and most experts advise against it. But what is not debatable is the fact that EVERY working set must be hard! If you're not struggling with the last couple reps of a set, that set was not a strength training set. At best, it was a warm-up set; at worst, it was a waste of time.

Another important factor in training is consistency. Admittedly, it can be difficult to consistently go to the gym. To help me, on days where I lack motivation, I'll just do something I don't mind. For example, I'll hit biceps, triceps, and/or chest instead of legs. My logic is simple: It's better to train the same muscle group twice in a few days than skip another workout. (Note: For most muscle groups, allow a minimum of one rest day between sessions targeting the same muscle group.) That said, obviously, don't use this tip too often as you need to be training your entire body on at least a semi-regular basis. Another tip is to use elective classes to help maintain a workout schedule, as many colleges offer health and/or fitness options for electives that will count towards your degree. I believe these classes can often be a better option than taking another class on a topic unrelated to your major. To be blunt, the knowledge gained from fitness classes will probably have a much greater positive impact on your life than other electives on topics you're not interested in. Lastly, don't be concerned with gaining too much muscle and getting too big. Getting big takes a conscious effort and a lot of hard work, and unless you're trying to get big, you won't.

Along with being an important part of the training process, a proper night's sleep – i.e., not during class – is another fantastic avenue to reducing stress. Yes, this can be difficult as insomnia is often a side effect of stress. Hence the importance of compounding the stress-reducing methods described in this book (working out, eating healthy, avoiding caffeine, etc.). These methods not only help reduce stress in their own right, but can also help facilitate a good night's sleep. If you combine these methods with a consistent sleep schedule and ensure your bedroom is dark and cool (60−67 °F [15.6−19.4 °C]), then you should be able to fall asleep naturally and quickly.[66] Other methods commonly recommended to improve sleep quality include sleeping in a quiet bedroom and not exposing yourself to blue light two to three hours before bed.[67, 68] Unfortunately, I tend not to follow these last two recommendations, as living in a modern society can make it difficult. For example, I use a fan as a white noise machine to drown out traffic and other urban noises.

If you don't believe sleep plays a role in reducing stress, consider a study published in 2021 that found those who averaged six hours or less of sleep per night were approximately two and a half times more likely to have frequent mental distress than those who averaged more than six hours of sleep.[69] Furthermore, sleep does far more than help reduce stress. In fact, I could have easily written about sleep in Chapter 9, the chapter on self-improvement, since getting a proper natural night's sleep every night is one of the best things you can do to improve both your physical and mental health. (I say "natural sleep" because sedation from drugs, such as alcohol, differs in a negative way from actual sleep and should be avoided.[70]) I could cite endless studies on the importance of sleep, but to save all of us time, I'll list just a few and hope that drives home the point. Athletes who sleep less than eight hours a night have an injury rate that is 1.7 times higher than those who get a full night's rest.[71] A test group had a 20% increase in speed and a 35% improvement in accuracy when learning a sequence on a keyboard, over the control group that was told to sleep less but practice more. Obtaining six hours or less of sleep can hasten the onset of physical exhaustion by up to 30%.[70]

If you still do not believe sleep is important, I get it, but please do your own research. I used to be one of those guys that thought it was manly and tough to not get a good night's sleep. I would say things like, "Aw, you don't need sleep, be a man." Now, a little older and, perhaps a little wiser, I realize how foolish I was and how importance sleep is, which is nicely summed up by this quote:

"Sleep is the greatest legal performance-enhancing drug that most people are probably neglecting in sport [this includes physical performance, learning, memory, etc.]."[70] Honestly, I don't know why everyone doesn't aim for the recommended seven to nine hours, as sleep is an enjoyable activity that significantly improves your overall quality of life. I know my day is remarkably better after a good night's sleep. On the other hand, days are rough and usually less productive when you're so tired that keeping your eyes open is a struggle (at least, without relying on caffeine or any other drug). For the sake of completeness, and because I don't want to scare you in the wrong direction, know that too much sleep isn't ideal either. In fact, both too much and too little sleep tend to lead to an earlier death.[72–74]

While the other methods discussed may seem more intuitive, having a positive attitude, even in the face of negativity, can also be a powerful stress reducer. A 2019 study analyzed the effects of positive thinking training on hemodialysis patients. The researchers found stress and anxiety decreased by 29.5% and 18%, respectively, while the patients' quality of life increased by 59.1%.[75] Thus, never underestimate the power of a positive attitude.

Last, but certainly not least, learn to say no. College life can be overwhelming, and it's impossible to do everything. Thus, make a conscious effort to recognize when it's necessary to say no. If you have an exam next week, stay home Friday night to study. If you have more homework than normal, and your boss wants you to work extra hours, kindly decline with an explanation of why you can't. Missing one night with your friends or a few extra hours at a job, especially if it doesn't pertain to your future career, will likely have zero long-term impact on your life. However, the consistent reduction in stress and, perhaps, better grades could very well have a long-term impact. Therefore, remember to prioritize and manage your schedule, and don't be afraid to turn down activities, or even some exciting opportunities, to free up extra time when needed.

Chapter Bullet Points

- Stop comparing yourself to others

- Organize and prioritize your time

- Stop worrying about a bad grade

- Maintain a healthy lifestyle

- Get seven to nine hours of sleep per night

- Saying no is a great time management strategy

Notes

_____

_____

_____

_____

_____

_____

11. Additional information

In this chapter, we will discuss topics I wanted to touch on but do not require a deep dive at this point in your educational career. Moreover, Appendix A has additional resources; your major will determine which ones are useful to you. Though, you should take a look at all of them. It would be unfortunate to miss out on a great resource for school or, perhaps, life.

11.1. Computer programming

I wanted to touch on computer programming due to the scary nature of it. At first sight, it can feel overwhelming; thankfully, it's nowhere near as hard as it appears. A common misconception is that learning to code is as hard as learning a second language. This is not true, as learning to code is far easier. I strongly believe that the only people who think learning a programming language is as hard as learning a second language are programmers that don't speak a second language.

Coding is actually relatively easy, especially to start. Think of it this way: Do you play a sport, an instrument, or have any skill in anything? Was it actually that hard to get started? Of course not; however, at first you weren't very good, and it probably took years to develop the skills you have today. Coding is similar, so start with a very small project. For example, use a for loop to count to ten and print the outputs to the screen. Then, build on that success with a slightly harder project. Before you know it, you'll be a far more skilled programmer than me. For help learning to program, one can use the countless online resources that are available; many, like YouTube, are FREE.

Once you get the hang of it, coding is actually enjoyable. In truth, if I could go back in time, I would seriously consider taking up computer science as my major. One thing you should do right now is look into Arduinos (and/or Raspberry Pi's). An Arduino is a micro-controller that allows you to create awesome projects. At this point, you should go ahead and YouTube cool Arduino projects (and/or Raspberry Pi projects). Watch out though, being a STEM major, you may get hooked, and using Arduinos may just become your new favorite hobby. Sorry for destroying all of your free time in advance.

Lastly, on a side note, any coders reading this should not freak out. I am not saying programmers are not highly skilled. Many absolutely are, and many do far more complex programming than I ever have. However, ego aside, was it really that hard to get started? Is it really that hard to use for loops and if statements as a foundation to create many programs? The answers: no and no.

11.2. Linux

People often believe they have two choices for their operating system: Windows or Mac. This is far from the truth, as there are many operating systems available, many of which are completely free. A significant number of these are built on the Linux kernel. (A kernel is an essential part of an operating system because it allocates machine resources to running programs.) Looking into Linux is worth your time and effort, especially if you are a computer science major. This is because Linux is frequently used in the computer science world. That said, there are advantages to Linux that could benefit everyone (e.g., it's lightweight, provides privacy, and is very customizable). There are an abundance of Linux distros to choose from (e.g., Mint, Ubuntu, openSUSE, Arch, or Gentoo), but beginners should probably start with user-friendly options like: Mint or Ubuntu.

Getting started with Linux is easy, too, as you can test drive Linux with little effort. This is through something called a virtual machine (e.g., VirtualBox). Basically, a virtual machine will use software instead of a physical computer to run an operating system. I won't go into more detail since there are endless resources about it online. But just know, you can install Linux on a virtual machine which leaves your current operating system intact. And yes, this can all be done for free. Your only cost is your time. Another option, if you want access to your current operating system, is dual booting your computer – i.e., having two operating systems on the same machine (e.g., Windows and a Linux distribution) without using a virtual machine. If you do this, you'll be able to select what operating system you want to use when your computer boots up.

I know many people believe Linux is this foreign operating system that no one uses, and that is semi-true for desktop computers, where Windows has a market share of roughly 73% (as of June 2024).[76] However, the Linux kernel (or a modified version of it) is extremely popular as it's in everything from phones (e.g., Android) and supercomputers to refrigerators and medical devices. There is a high probability that you interact with some form of the Linux kernel every day. To drive home this point, here are some interesting facts to highlight the popularity of the Linux kernel: Since 2018, the top 500 of the world's supercomputers all use Linux.[77] As of 2020, an estimated 96% of the top one million websites run on Linux-based servers; the majority of Amazon's cloud computing platform (Amazon EC2) runs on Linux at 94%; and even 60% of Microsoft's cloud computing platform (Azure) runs on Linux.[78]

11.3. Final thoughts

1. I barely used spreadsheet programs in college (Excel, Google Sheets, etc.). However, many companies run on spreadsheets, and countless STEM majors' careers will involve using spreadsheets regularly. Therefore, it is a good idea to try to incorporate them into your college career, even if they're not required. You may even be surprised by how useful they are, as spreadsheet programs are more feature-rich than most people realize. A few helpful features that I frequently use include conditional formatting and programming terms (e.g., if statements, and statements, ceiling, pi, and sum). But these programs can be far more complex; for example, in Excel, you can use Macros and Visual Basic Analysis (VBA). Macros provide a way to automate tasks, and VBA is Microsoft's programming language for their Office applications.

2. While it shouldn't matter – because many in the field know that mechanical engineering and aerospace engineering degrees are essentially equivalent – a mechanical engineering degree may open more doors than an aerospace engineering degree. During the interview process, I often had to explain to recruiters that the degrees are equivalent. And while I'll never know, I would guess I have been passed over for jobs because I had an aerospace engineering degree instead of a mechanical engineering degree. (This was before I graduated with a PhD in

mechanical engineering.) A good way to understand the advantage of a mechanical engineering degree would be to browse online job postings for engineering positions. You will notice many jobs just list mechanical engineering as the preferred degree. On the other hand, most of the aerospace engineering job postings clearly state "aerospace engineering, mechanical engineering, or an equivalent degree." That said, you will still have many opportunities as an aerospace engineer, and many mechanical engineering job postings do say "or an equivalent degree." Regardless, it is just something to be mindful of if your main goal is simply to land an engineering job, and you're not too picky on the exact role or industry. Though, if your heart is set on becoming an aerospace engineer, then, of course, an aerospace engineering degree would offer a slight edge over a mechanical engineering degree.

3. An Engineering Technology degree is not equivalent to a Bachelor of Science in Engineering degree. (For instance, a degree in "Mechanical Engineering Technology" is not equivalent to a degree in "Mechanical Engineering.") While some companies will treat the degrees as interchangeable, others will not. I have seen some companies specifically state in job postings that those with "Engineering Technology" degrees will not be considered qualified for the opening. For the majority, a Bachelor of Science in Engineering is the preferred degree. That said, technology degrees still offer great career opportunities, especially for those who want to be more hands on. Make sure to research both to choose the right one for you.

4. Computers have been around a long time and are only growing in our everyday use. Because of that, it's worth the time and

effort for most STEM majors to learn more about computers and how they function. This is especially true for computer science majors. I'm not saying you need to become an expert, but one should have a general understanding of what role the CPU, GPU, RAM, and drive all play within the computer. By understanding their roles, you'll have a better understanding of what your needs are. For example, there is a common myth that more RAM makes your PC faster. That's only true if you don't have enough RAM. Often the root cause of a PC running slow, if it's a RAM issue, is because your RAM is maxed out. When that happens, the computer has to move some of the information stored on the RAM to the drive. (It's called paging or swapping depending on your operating system.) The issue is, the CPU can pull data significantly faster from RAM than a drive. Therefore, if your computer has to access data that has been moved to the drive, your computer will slow down. However, if you only use eight gigabytes of RAM but your computer has sixteen, all (or most) of your data will stay in the RAM. Consequently, buying more RAM will not make your PC run faster and will be a waste of money.

On top of avoiding unnecessary expenses, understanding the roles of computer components can also help you diagnose many issues with your PC. This will allow you to answer questions, such as:

- Why did my computer crash after I opened the 500th tab in my internet browser?

- Why does this large file take so long to open?

- Why does my computer lag so much when working within that large file?

- What computer component(s) will I need to upgrade to fix both those large file issues?

- For my next PC, what parts can I save money on that won't hurt the overall performance of the PC for my use cases?

- Do I even need a GPU?

- Why does my computer turn on those annoying fans when using this program but not that program?

5. Your professors know that Chegg exists. They also know students blindly copy Chegg and/or solution manuals. This isn't a secret. In fact, in the Dynamics class I taught at Western Michigan University, I chose a problem that the solution manual had incorrect. I even told the class about the incorrect solution, and openly admitted it took me longer than it should have to realize the solution was wrong. Truth be told, it probably took around five minutes of staring at the "solution," confused, until it dawned on me, this is a solution to a completely different problem. When telling this to the class, I made the joke, "I should ask this question on the homework just to see how many people will still copy it." Well, I did ask, and out of 66 students, I had three or four copy the incorrect "solution" for their homework. Needless to say, they received zeros. Moral of the story: don't cheat.

If you are going to use Chegg or a solution manual, that's fine as no one can stop you. But please use them as a study aid/homework helper. Do not blindly copy the solution, as it will only cause problems down the road. This is because when viewing a solution, the problem looks easier than it is. Therefore, you might convince yourself that you can easily solve that type of problem on an exam. This mindset is often what leads students to the justification that copying the solution is acceptable. However, I promise that it won't look so easy on an exam. If you don't believe me, try it yourself. Review the problem solution, then a few days later attempt the problem without the solution by your side. Without the solution manual, was it as easy as it seemed? Probably not, and that's precisely the issue. Now imagine how difficult encountering a completely different, yet similar type, problem on the exam would be.

This phenomenon is common during exam reviews as well. For example, have you ever had a teacher go over an exam problem, and you think to yourself, "How did I get that wrong? It was so easy?" The truth is, it isn't that easy. If it was, you would have got the answer correct. The solution may seem easy because the steps are laid out clearly. However, the hard part of a problem is knowing what steps to take and what equations to use in the first place. Once the steps and equations to solve a problem are laid out, solving the problem becomes trivial and often nothing more than plug and chug. Thus, the ultimate goal of homework isn't to torture students. (That's just a bonus for teachers.) The ultimate goal is to throw enough different problems at them so by exam time the steps required to solve these problems are so ingrained that the problems feel as easy as they appear. Hence, the importance of doing homework independently, without relying on Chegg, solution manuals, or AI.

6. AI programs, such as ChatGPT, are powerful, useful tools, and the more tools you have in your tool belt, the better. However, there is always going to be a debate on what is ethical and

what is not with regard to their use. Hence, some choose to avoid them, which is a valid option to consider depending on your stance on the issue. With that said, here's my take: If you use them to write for you (paragraphs, entire reports, etc.), I believe that clearly qualifies as plagiarism, even if you're not technically copying directly from another human.

However, there are ways to integrate these tools into your writing without plagiarizing. The first is to use them as a thesaurus (or a phrasebook). To do this, simply enter prompts like these: "other words for additionally" or "other ways to say: On a side note." If the AI doesn't give you any examples you like, you can simply ask for more (e.g., enter: "give 5 more examples"). The second is using AI to check for grammar or other writing errors. This is as straightforward as entering prompts similar to these: "is the grammar correct in this sentence: ___YOUR SENTENCE___," "is this a complete sentence: ___YOUR SENTENCE___," "should _____ be capitalized in this sentence: ___YOUR SENTENCE___," or, even, "grammar? ___YOUR SENTENCE___." If your sentence was grammatically incorrect, AI may output a corrected sentence without telling you what was wrong. To save time, just ask the AI what was changed (e.g., enter: "what did you change?"). AI will also tell you why something needs to be changed. If it doesn't, again simply ask the AI program why the change is necessary. (It's important to understand what was changed and why, since you need to be learning and not just directly copying.)

You can also use AI to enhance the overall quality of your sentences; though, ethically, this may fall into a gray area, at least when it comes to writing papers. But I believe if you use AI to give you ideas to improve your sentences, and don't just copy, then it is acceptable. Here's an example, if you enter this into the prompt: "give 5 examples of this written better: __YOUR SENTENCE__," then AI will give you five versions of that sentence. (Often, I don't even put in the entire sentence, just the part I need help with.) Instead of picking one of those five sentences and copying it, review all of them to help you think of a way to improve your original sentence. Using AI like this, I would argue, is not much different than using normal tools such as a thesaurus. Nevertheless, I don't suggest you do this approach for every sentence. Not only would that be too time-consuming, but at a certain point, you may be crossing into unethical territory. Thus, I would suggest using this method sparingly, only when you are struggling to get those pesky sentences to flow naturally, or the sentence quality is not up to your preferred standard.

Here are a couple of other ways I recommend using AI. First, utilize AI to help with transitions. You can do this by entering prompts like: "How to transition between __YOUR SENTENCE #1 __ and __YOUR SENTENCE #2 __" or "How to transition into this sentence to start a paragraph: __YOUR SENTENCE__." Secondly, you can use AI to help find more appropriate words. For example, instead of using the term "baby deer," you could enter a prompt like: "What's a better term than baby deer?" (Answer: Fawn). Thus, just make sure you utilize AI programs as learning tools to enhance your writing, rather than relying on them to do the writing for you.

If you do choose to use AI, know AI is not perfect. These

AI programs can and will output wrong information, so use them with caution. I semi-regularly end up double-checking AI's output with a regular Google search. Moreover, at the end of the day, your professor and college have final say. If they say don't use AI, then don't use AI. Lastly, there are a couple of important things to note with regard to the use of AI. First, everything you input into an AI prompt is likely to be saved and could be used by the AI in the future. Therefore, it's probably wise to avoid using AI with classified information. Secondly, using AI may limit your growth as a writer, as the feedback you receive on college essays and reports may not be based on your natural writing ability.

7. As you leave adolescence and transition into adulthood, it's time to understand the differences between an opinion (i.e., an idea coming from someone without experience) and advice (i.e., an idea coming from someone with experience), and why it is important to gather opinions and/or advice from multiple sources. This topic was briefly discussed previously in Chapters 2 and 4, with regard to parents and teachers; however, the subject is more complex than just having and not having experience. Hence, the importance of elaborating further here. An opinion is relatively straight forward; it is an idea from someone without experience. (This is especially true if they also lack regular interactions with those who do have experience.) Basically, the person has little to no background with the subject matter at hand. That person has nothing more than an opinion. I am by no means knocking opinions. We all have them, and if you don't have experience, you have to start somewhere. Plus, an opinion from someone who knows

you may still provide relevant information on how you should proceed. All I'm trying to say is that opinions are the lowest form of help, and opinions should be used with caution. There is a reason why this quote by L. H. Hardwick is popular: "A man with experience is never at the mercy of a man with an opinion."

Advice, on the other hand, is more complicated. Someone's experience may not be relevant to you, as you could have completely different paths. For example, if you are receiving advice on how to earn acceptance into an elite college from a wealthy legacy, and you come from a poor, non-college-educated family, the advice, "Don't worry about your grades; just have your dad talk to the dean to get in," probably won't help you too much. Obviously, that example was a bit exaggerated, but I hope you see the point. If you don't, here's a real-world example. When I got my first engineering job offer, I told someone I trust heavily that I thought it was a bit low, and I was going to try and negotiate a higher salary. While the offer was far more money than I have ever made, it was still on the low side for a starting mechanical engineering role. That person warned me not to negotiate, saying I could lose the job offer. Well, I did negotiate and got myself a nearly 16% pay increase to start. I know with all my heart, the advice from that person had zero malicious intent. They were trying to give me the best advice they possibly could. Unfortunately, that advice was still bad. Why? Because he was a blue-collar worker, and in his world at the company where he worked, it was mostly a matter of either taking the money they offered or being replaced by someone else who will. So, the person I received the advice from was literally trying to stop me from losing the job offer. It was fantastic advice from their point of view, and it was formed by their experiences. However, I was applying for a white-collar job, something that person lacked experience in, and admittedly, so did I at the time. But I did enough research to know it was a lowball offer, so I went with my gut, and yes, I worried that I might lose the offer. Thankfully, though, it worked out well for me. (Here's a tip: When negotiating a salary for a white-collar job, try to get the company to give the first number. This will likely be the minimum salary, close to it, or a range they're willing to offer for the role. If it's one of the first two options, they almost always have room to increase it. Thus, do your research and always counter at a higher, but realistic, value. If they provide a range, then again, do your research and justify to them why you deserve more than the bottom of that range. NOTE: Salary research needs to be done before the interview to ensure you're prepared.)

Anyways, when you are accumulating advice and ideas from someone, make sure to recognize the differences between their path and yours. This highlights the importance of seeking advice from multiple sources, since paths are never exactly the same, and advice has a spectrum of helpfulness. This spectrum includes advice from people who don't know you and have had a different path in life than you, as well as from those who know you best and share a similar life path. And, of course, there are those who give you bad advice on purpose, for whatever ridiculous reason they may have, such as seeing you as competition or simply not liking you. Nevertheless, outside of those people, all the opinions and advice you receive have some merit. It's just up to you to determine how to apply, or when not to apply, the information you receive to your situation.

All that to say, you're a young adult now, and you have to take responsibility for your life and think for yourself. You should no longer be blaming others for your mistakes. It's your life and your decisions. When you (temporarily) fail at something due to receiving bad advice, remember it's still YOUR fault because you did not do enough homework before making the decision. It is NOT the fault of the person who gave you the advice. Regardless, every failed opportunity is nothing more than a learning opportunity, and a chance to add experience you can rely on to make decisions in the future. It can often be failed experiences that truly shape who you are. As you consider this, I'd also emphasize to always be nice when receiving an opinion or advice. In most cases, it is someone trying their best to help you with the knowledge they have, and at the end of the day, that's all you can ask for.

8. For many students, college is the first time they will be living without their parents. While this newfound freedom may appear nice, it comes with drawbacks, such as budgeting for the first time or taking on significantly more responsibilities. With regard to budgeting, I won't go into detail on how one should budget, as that is not the focal point of this book. However, I do find it important to talk about money and budgeting because, whether you like it or not, money is an important aspect of life and it should be taken seriously. Unfortunately, the ability to budget well and not live paycheck to paycheck is uncommon, as evidenced by the fact that 63% of Americans were living paycheck to paycheck as of November 2022.[79] But for those who learn to budget, avoid spending every dime they earn, and save for the future, life will be much easier. If you

weren't raised with these habits, you need to start developing them now. It will drastically improve your college experience, and, frankly, the rest of your life. Plus, college is the perfect time to start, as most of you only have to worry about yourself (i.e., you don't have spouses or kids).

A good starting point, and in many cases, a good ending point, is looking into Dave Ramsey. He would be my recommended first research source for any young adult with a desire to learn about how to handle money. Though, I do highly encourage looking into other financial experts because, like most things in life, there is no one correct way to handle finances, only preferred ways. The more you learn, the more you can adapt your financial plan to suit the life you want to live. (Of course, be wise when researching other financial experts and focus on those with a proven track record of success. Keep in mind that most on social media do not qualify as experts, and their advice should be avoided.)

On top of researching on your own, you can also use your college elective classes to increase your financial literacy. This includes classes on the stock market, where you'll learn about topics like mutual funds, which are a great way to build long-term wealth. Even if you don't start investing until after college – which is typical and perfectly acceptable for most college students – it's beneficial to begin learning how to invest, and perhaps more importantly, why you should invest. Learning now will just put you ahead of the curve when it's time for you to start investing, such as when you start working full-time. At the end of the day, by the time you leave college, you should no longer have the excuse of, "I didn't realize I was bad with money because no one taught me how to handle it." "You" need to teach you how!

9. Throughout this book, we've touched on the importance of creating systems, and I want to revisit the topic one last time since having systems in place can dramatically increase your chances of success. For example, one system I use to maintain a healthier lifestyle is rarely buying unhealthy food for my home. If the unhealthy food isn't in my house, I can't eat it. If it is in the home, I know myself, and I will eat a ton of it. For some reason I have little self-control at home but a ton of self-control at the grocery store. Plus, keeping the majority of my diet healthy allows me to occasionally eat unhealthy food when I'm out with friends and family, without any guilt. This system has allowed me to, for the most part, maintain my weight without too much effort. Therefore, consider the goals and objectives you have in your life and think of ways to implement systems that can help you succeed!

You did it! You read my book, and for that, I want to personally thank you! This book did not happen overnight; it took years to write. I wrote most of it, perhaps stupidly, while working as a full-time engineer and a PhD candidate. I probably should have finished my PhD before writing a book, but I didn't. Needless to say, a lot of blood, sweat, and tears went into the making of this book. Therefore, I truly appreciate every single person who takes time out of their busy lives to read it. If you have any questions, you're welcome to contact me through my website.

All I have left are two small requests: If you found this book useful and informative, please share it with friends and family who might benefit from it – or just send them a link to buy it or to my website:

JustinRittenhousePhD.com. Additionally, I would appreciate it if you left a review online, as it helps others discover it too. I'm not some big corporation. I'm literally just a dude trying to help and teach future generations how to succeed. And to do that, I could use all the help you're willing to give to get my book out there. Thank You!

Chapter Bullet Points

- Computer programming is easier than it appears

- Practice using spreadsheet programs in college

- Learn the functions of major computer components

- YOU are responsible for your successes and failures in life

- Learning how to budget is important in college and life

Notes

A. Resources

You'll naturally come across many resources during your academic career. I tried to avoid listing those; the goal was to give resources that you may never stumble across. My hope is to provide all STEM majors with at least a couple of new resources. Lastly, note that a great way to find free alternatives to costly proprietary software is simply searching "open source alternatives for NAME OF PROPRIETARY SOFTWARE" into your favorite search engine.

The author's website

Justin Rittenhouse (JustinRittenhousePhD.com):

> I plan on regularly updating my site to provide useful tools and information (ranging from engineering tools to job search insights and everything in between).

Resources to help with homework

WolframAlpha (wolframalpha.com):

> While WolframAlpha can do more, it's a fantastic tool for math homework, especially for those without a fancy calculator. I used it quite a bit.

MIT OpenCourseWare (ocw.mit.edu):

> Massachusetts Institute of Technology hosts classes from its own faculty for free.

Resources for writing papers

Google Scholar (scholar.google.com):

> Google Scholar works similarly to normal Google; however, it searches scholarly literature. Thus, it is a great tool for finding quality sources when working on research projects or papers.

LibreOffice (libreoffice.org):

> LibreOffice is a free and open-source office suite. (Basically, free versions of Word, PowerPoint, Excel, etc.)

Okular (okular.kde.org):

> A free and open-source tool for working with PDFs. Features include highlighting, commenting, underlining text, popup notes, signature support, and more.

LaTeX (latex-project.org):

> A document preparation system for creating high-quality documents such as technical papers. Note: This book was written in LaTeX.

Texmaker (xm1math.net/texmaker):

> My preferred LaTeX editor. (Note: TeXstudio is popular as well.)

JabRef (jabref.org):

> JabRef is a citation and reference management tool. It's a great way to edit, store, and organize citations for LaTeX documents.

Programming resources

Google's Python Class (developers.google.com/edu/python):

There is a little bit of pre-programming knowledge expected. However, if you are a beginner, this is a great way to improve your Python skills.

Anaconda (anaconda.com):

If you program in Python or R, this is a great tool. While I do not use Anaconda with Linux (it is compatible), I do typically use it with Windows.

Octave (gnu.org/software/octave):

An open-source alternative to MATLAB with similar syntax.

Arduino (arduino.cc):

A great (and cheap) way to start coding with hardware.

Raspberry Pi (raspberrypi.org):

Ditto to Arduino, but it costs more. I'll let you do your homework on their differences.

Vim (vim.org):

A free and open-source text editor with a fantastic command-line interface.

gedit (help.gnome.org/users/gedit/stable):

My GUI based text editor of choice.

Other useful resources

Syncthing (syncthing.net):

A great way to have synchronization of folders between devices.

FreeCAD (freecad.org):

A free and open-source CAD program.

Tinkercad (tinkercad.com):

A free, web browser-based 3D modeling program includes some great features, such as an Arduino simulator.

CalculiX (calculix.de):

A free and open-source finite element program with input files similar to Abaqus.

Gmsh (gmsh.info):

A free and open-source finite element mesh generator.

ParaView (paraview.org):

A fantastic tool for analyzing and visualizing data. For example, post-processing computer simulations (e.g., finite or discrete element models).

VirtualBox (virtualbox.org):

VirtualBox makes it easy to run one operating system within another. It has many use cases, such as running Linux on a computer where dual-booting isn't an option, and it's also fantastic for experimenting with other operating systems (e.g., different Linux distributions). Plus, it's free and open-source.

Shutter (shutter-project.org):

A feature-rich open-source alternative to Microsoft's Snipping Tool.

WineHQ (winehq.org):

Allows Windows applications – including games – to run in Linux. Of course, it's free and open-source, too.

OBS Studio (obsproject.com):

A free and open-source video recording and live streaming program.

Bibliography

1. Michael T. Nietzel. New from U.S. Census Bureau: Number of Americans with a bachelor's degree continues to grow, Feb 2021.

2. National Center for Education Statistics. Income of young adults. Online.

3. U.S. Department of Education. Beginning college students who change their majors within 3 years of enrollment. Online, December 2017.

4. LinkedIn Corporate Communications. Eighty-percent of professionals consider networking important to career success. Online, June 2017.

5. Sungki Hong and Devin Werner. How many people does it take to start a company? Online, July 2020.

6. Michael J. Handel. What do people do at work? *Journal for Labour Market Research*, 49, October 2016.

7. Kim Rosenkoetter Powell, Elena Lytkina Botelho, and Vamsi Tetali. How CEOs without college degrees got to the top. Online, February 2018.

8. Ramsey. The national study of millionaires. Online, April 2021.

9. Deniz Çam. Doctorate, degree or dropout: How much education it takes to become a billionaire. Online, October 2017.

10. Brianna McGurran and Alicia Hahn. College tuition inflation: Compare the cost of college over time. Online, March 2022.

11. J Geiman. The psychological toll of student debt. Online, October 2021.

12. Victoria Wang. Killer loans — college debt triggers depression and suicide. Online, June 2019.

13. Melanie Hanson. Average cost of college [2021]: Yearly tuition expenses. Online, May 2024.

14. Melanie Hanson. Average cost of community college [2021]: Tuition fees. Online, October 2023.

15. U.S. News. Best national university rankings. Online, September 2023.

16. payscale.com. Best universities and colleges by salary potential. Online, 2024.

17. Melanie Hanson. How do people pay for college? Online, October 2021.

18. Mark C. Perna. $100 million in scholarship money goes unclaimed every year. Does it have to? Online, November 2021.

19. Philip Guo. Python is now the most popular introductory teaching language at top U.S. universities. Online, July 2017.

20. Brian Eastwood. The 10 most popular programming languages to learn in 2022. Online, June 2018.

21. Vanshika Kakkar. Top 10 programming languages to learn in 2022. Online, January 2022.

22. Berkeley Extension. 11 most in-demand programming languages in 2021. Online, Feb 2021.

23. geeksforgeeks.org. Top 10 programming languages that will rule in 2021, Dec 2020.

24. Sruthi Veeraraghavan. Best programming languages to learn in 2021, Apr 2021.

25. Saurabh Tyagi. How Fortune 500 is embracing open source technology. Online, July 2016.

26. Justin Rittenhouse. *Development of a discrete element model for artificial turf.* Dissertations, Western Michigan University, April 2024.

27. Peter Gustafson, Andrew Geeslin, and James Jastifer. An open source reverse engineering workflow: Geometry to optimization. In *57th AIAA/ASCE/AHS/ASC Structures, Structural Dynamics, and Materials Conference*, 2016.

28. Justin Rittenhouse. Investigation of discrete element methods for stud to turf interactions. Online, April 2018.

29. Brad Plumer. Only 27 percent of college grads have a job related to their major. Online, May 2013.

30. Jim Harter. Employee engagement on the rise in the U.S. Online, August 2018.

31. Christa Sgobba. Here's when you're most and least likely to have a heart attack. Online, July 2017.

32. Casey Gale. Where did all the entry-level jobs go? Online, May 2021.

33. Julia Freeland Fisher. How to get a job often comes down to one elite personal asset, and many people still don't realize it. Online, December 2019.

34. Dana Guterman. To intern or not to intern: Which companies require an internship? Online, December 2019.

35. Josh Sanburn. How to make your resume last longer than 6 seconds. Online, Apr 2012.

36. Kelsey Purcell. Do I need a cover letter? Our survey results may surprise you. Online, November 2024.

37. Recruiting Daily Advisor Editorial Staff. Rejecting a job candidate because of body language. Online, May 2018.

38. Tracy Brower. 5 best ways to prepare for your interview so you get the job. Online, February 2023.

39. Lisa Hagendorf. Thanks, but no thanks: 68% of hiring managers say ungrateful job seekers are jeopardizing their own candidacy. Online, November 2017.

40. Jenifer Kuadli. 30 hiring statistics we can learn from. Online, February 2021.

41. Patrick V. Valtin. Why you need to hire more for soft skills and less for experience. Online, September 2019.

42. Lisa Fritscher. Glossophobia or the fear of public speaking. Online, July 2021.

43. Izz Scott LaMagdeleine. Did Wright brothers fly same year NYT said flying machines could take 10m years to develop? Online, May 2023.

44. Trafft.com. Time management statistics and facts that will surprise you. Online, April 2021.

45. Gravityflow.io. Why lost time seriously affects your profitability. Online.

46. Ecampusontario.pressbooks.pub. How graph misrepresents data. Online.

47. Wil. How many words are in the English language? Online, Jun 2020.

48. Douglas N. Arnold. The sinking of the Sleipner A offshore platform. Online, September 2009.

49. NASA. Earth our home planet. Online, December 2019.

50. The Open University. Is there any gravity on the ISS? Online.

51. Team Tony. Go from ordinary to extraordinary. Online.

52. Joan C. Williams, Saravanan Kesavan, and Lisa McCorkell. Research: When retail workers have stable schedules, sales and productivity go up. Online, March 2018.

53. Nir Eyal. Have we been thinking about willpower the wrong way for 30 years? Online, November 2016.

54. Phillippa Lally, Cornelia H. M. van Jaarsveld, Henry W. W. Potts, and Jane Wardle. How are habits formed: Modelling habit formation in the real world. *European Journal of Social Psychology*, 40(6):998–1009, 2010.

55. ISS National Laboratory. History and timeline of the ISS. Online.

56. Inga Usher, Peter Hellyer, Keng Siang Lee, Robert Leech, Adam Hampshire, Alexander Alamri, and Aswin Chari. "It's not rocket science" and "It's not brain surgery"—"It's a walk in the park": prospective comparative study. *BMJ*, 375, November 2021.

57. Maxim Dsouza. The astonishing success story of the genius Polgár sisters. Online.

58. Abigail Abrams. Yes, impostor syndrome is real. Here's how to deal with it. Online, June 2018.

59. Liberty Clearwater. Understanding the science behind learning retention. Online, January 2022.

60. University of Michigan Health. Healthy eating to decrease stress. Online, August 2020.

61. Simone Radavelli-Bagatini, Lauren C. Blekkenhorst, Marc Sim, Richard L. Prince, Nicola P. Bondonno, Catherine P. Bondonno, Richard Woodman, Reindolf Anokye, James Dimmock, Ben Jackson, Leesa Costello, Amanda Devine, Mandy J. Stanley, Joanne M. Dickson, Dianna J. Magliano, Jonathan E. Shaw, Robin M. Daly, Jonathan M. Hodgson, and Joshua R. Lewis. Eating more fruit and vegetables linked to less stress, study finds. Online, May 2021.

62. Urska Dobersek, Kelsey Teel, Sydney Altmeyer, Joshua Adkins, Gabrielle Wy, and Jackson Peak. Meat and mental health: A meta-analysis of meat consumption, depression, and anxiety. *Critical Reviews in Food Science and Nutrition*, 63(19):3556–3573, 2023. PMID: 34612096.

63. Nicole L. Mihalopoulos, Peggy Auinger, and Jonathan D. Klein.

The freshman 15: Is it real? *J Am Coll Health*, 56(5):531–533, September 2008.

64. National Institute on Alcohol Abuse and Alcoholism. The link between stress and alcohol. Online, 2012.

65. Jeff Haden. Science says strength training twice a week dramatically reduces anxiety stress. Online.

66. Norma Rabago. A cold room, not a warm bath, encourages sleep. Online, March 2023.

67. Jay Summer and Abhinav Singh. How noise can affect your sleep satisfaction. Online, March 2024.

68. Rob Newsom and Abhinav Singh. Blue light: What it is and how it affects sleep. Online, January 2024.

69. Amanda Blackwelder, Mikhail Hoskins, and Larissa Huber. Effect of inadequate sleep on frequent mental distress. Online, June 2021.

70. Matthew Walker. #1109 - Matthew Walker. Podcast, April 2018.

71. Lauren Garforth. Could sleep be the most powerful performance-enhancing drug? Online, May 2019.

72. Yeonju Kim, Lynne R. Wilkens, Susan M. Schembre, Brian E. Henderson, Laurence N. Kolonel, and Marc T. Goodman. Insufficient and excessive amounts of sleep increase the risk of premature death from cardiovascular and other diseases: The multiethnic cohort study. *Preventive Medicine*, 57(4):377–385, 2013.

73. Deborah L. Wingard and Lisa F. Berkman. Mortality Risk Associated with Sleeping Patterns Among Adults. *Sleep*, 6(2):102–107, 09 1983.

74. Hassan Khan, Danesh Kella, Setor K. Kunutsor, Kai Savonen, and Jari A. Laukkanen. Sleep duration and risk of fatal coronary heart disease, sudden cardiac death, cancer death, and all-cause mortality. *The American Journal of Medicine*, 131(12):1499–1505.e2, 2018.

75. Nasrin Shokrpour, Shima Sheidaie, Mehdi Amirkhani, Leila Bazrafkan, and Ameneh Modreki. Effect of positive thinking training on stress, anxiety, depression, and quality of life among hemodialysis patients: A randomized controlled clinical trial. Online, June 2021.

76. Statcounter Global Stats. Desktop operating system market share worldwide. Online, June 2024.

77. Abhishek Prakash. Linux runs all of the top 500 fastest supercomputers. Online, Nov 2020.

78. Jason Moth. Fascinating linux facts and statistics you need to know about. Online, 2020.

79. Jessica Dickler. Share of americans living paycheck to paycheck rises to 63% — here's how to get your finances back on track. Online, December 2022.

www.ingramcontent.com/pod-product-compliance
Lightning Source LLC
Chambersburg PA
CBHW021225130626
46554CB00004B/1369